TRANSFORMATIONAL GROWTH: INTERCULTURAL LEADERSHIP DISCIPLESHIP MENTORSHIP

Enoch Wan, Mark Hedinger, and Jon Raibley

Relational Paradigm Series of CDRR

Transformational Growth: Intercultural Leadership, Discipleship, Mentorship

Copyright 2023 © Western Academic Publishers

Enoch Wan, Mark Hedinger, Jon Raibley

Cover designed by Mark Benec

ISBN: 978-1-954692-18-3

CDRR (Center of Diaspora & Relational Research) @ https://www.westernseminary.edu/outreach/center-diaspora-relational-research

Western Academic Publishers

TABLE OF CONTENTS

LIST OF FIGURES v

SECTION 1 BASIC UNDERSTANDINGS 3

CHAPTER 1 Introduction 3

CHAPTER 2 Theoretical Foundations of Relational Intercultural Transformation 9

CHAPTER 3 Thematic Understanding of Intercultural Transformational Growth 23

SECTION 2 TRANSFORMATIONAL GROWTH: INTERCULTURAL LEADERSHIP 35

CHAPTER 4 Intercultural Leadership Introduction 37

CHAPTER 5 *Being* in Intercultural Leadership 59

CHAPTER 6 *Belonging* in Intercultural Leadership 65

CHAPTER 7 *Becoming* in Intercultural Leadership 71

SECTION 3 TRANSFORMATIONAL GROWTH: INTERCULTURAL DISCIPLESHIP 79

CHAPTER 8 Intercultural Discipleship Introduction 81

CHAPTER 9 *Being* in Intercultural Discipleship (Considers the question, "Who all are involved in Discipleship?") 87

CHAPTER 10 *Belonging* in Intercultural Discipleship 97

CHAPTER 11 *Becoming* in Intercultural Discipleship 109

CHAPTER 12 Discipleship Summary 119

SECTION 4 TRANSFORMATIONAL GROWTH: INTERCULTURAL MENTORSHIP 123

CHAPTER 13 Relational Intercultural Mentoring Introduction 125

CHAPTER 14 *Being* in Intercultural Mentoring 133

CHAPTER 15 Belonging in Intercultural Mentoring 141

CHAPTER 16 *Becoming* in Intercultural Mentoring 153

CHAPTER 17 Intercultural Mentoring Summary 163

CHAPTER 18 Conclusion 165

BIBLIOGRAPHY 167

LIST OF FIGURES

Figure 2-1. Distinction and Progression of Disciplinarities 9
Figure 2-2. Distinction and Progression of "Interculturality" 10
Figure 2-3. Relational Frameworks 11
Figure 2-4. Multi-level, Multi-dimension, Multi-stage of Relationship 13
Figure 2-5. Transformational Change Equation 14
Figure 2-6. The Process of Transformational Growth 14
Figure 2-7. Relational Intercultural Transformational Change........................16
Figure 2-8. Components of Relationship 17
Figure 2-9. New Testament "One Another" Commands and Developmental
Dimensions 19
Figure 2-10. The Roles of Influence and Choice 20
Figure 2-11. Examples of Transgressional and Transformational Changes
Within the Learning Domains..20
Figure 3-1. Assumptions in Relational Intercultural Ministry........................25
Figure 3-2. Approaches to Relational Intercultural Education 28
Figure 3-3. Communication Patterns: The Trinity...29
Figure 3-4. Communication Patterns: Creator and People 29
Figure 3-5. Communication Patterns in Monocultural Contexts 29
Figure 3-6. Communication Patterns in Intercultural Contexts........................30
Figure 3-7. The Umbrella Model: Christ-Centered Unity..................................31
Figure 3-8. Relational Training for Transformative Change: Dimensions &
Aspects 32
Figure 3-9. Program Outcomes of Training for Transformational Change 32
Figure 4-1. Relationally Transformational Leadership: Formation (Being)........41
Figure 4-2. Relationally Transformational Leadership: Performance (Doing) ..42
Figure 4-3. Two Christian Paradigms: Popular and Relationally Transformative
....46
Figure 4-4. Programmatic/Managerial/Entrepreneur & Relationally
Transformative Changes...48
Figure 4-5. Popular Approaches vs. Relationally Transformational Leadership at
Two Levels 50
Figure 4-6. Dimensions of Leadership in Operation...51
Figure 4-7. Narrative Framework and Transformational Change 52
Figure 4-8. Relational Transformational Leadership for Change in two
Dimensions. 53
Figure 4-9. The Practice and Process of Relational Intercultural Leadership 54

Figure 4-10. Two Types of Change: Relationally Transgressive and Transformative..55
Figure 4-11. Relationally Transgressive and Transformative Changes at Two Levels..56
Figure 5-1. Multi-layers Narrative of Intercultural Leadership 60
Figure 5-2. Intercultural Leadership in Action...61
Figure 6-1. From Ethnocentrism to Ethno-relationality 67
Figure 6-2. Relational Realism and Transformational Change.....................68
Figure 6-3. Intercultural Leadership in Action...69
Figure 7-1. The Process and Outcome of Transformational Growth in Intercultural Leadership 72
Figure 8-1. Relational Intercultural Development in Discipleship 83
Figure 8-2. Comparing Discipleship from Programmatic and Relational Approaches 84
Figure 8-3. Jesus' Relational Training in Matthew's Gospel........................84
Figure 8-4. Comparing Leadership Paradigms: Popular vs Relational...........85
Figure 9-1. Relational Training for Transformative Change: Dimensions & Aspects...88
Figure 9-2. Examples of Some Variables that Distinguish Humans from One Another..89
Figure 9-3. Variables that Distinguish Created Spirit Beings 89
Figure 9-4. Variables that Distinguish One Member of Triune God from Others 89
Figure 9-5. Discipleship Community, by Generation 90
Figure 9-6. Multi-layers of Intercultural Discipleship................................92
Figure 9-7. Life Transitions and Related Discipleship Opportunities............94
Figure 10-1. Intercultural Discipleship in Action................................... 107
Figure 11-1. Holistic Outcomes for Discipleship 110
Figure 11-2. Popular Approaches vs. Relationally Transformational Discipleship at Two Levels 112
Figure 11-3. Relational Transformation 115
Figure 11-4. Five Steps of Relational Convergence 117
Figure 11-5. Intercultural Discipleship in Action................................... 118
Figure 13-1. Transformational Development in Mentorship...................... 126
Figure 13-2. Conceptual model of the relationship between cultural awareness and intercultural mentoring relationships. 129
Figure 13-3. Aspects of Cultural Awareness.. 130
Figure 14-1. Examples of Cultural Values.. 134
Figure 14-2. Chan's List of Cultural Influences..................................... 134
Figure 14-3. Functioning from Your Core as a Child of God 137
Figure 14-4. Elements in the Learner-Centered Mentoring Paradigm.......... 138

Figure 14-5. Three critical formations 139
Figure 15-1. Chan's Key Elements of Mentoring 147
Figure 15-2. Relational Spiritual Mentorship Process 149
Figure 15-3. Deepening Connections in Distance Mentoring.......... 150
Figure 16-1. Leaders Who Finish Poorly and Those Who Finish Well.............. 154
Figure 16-2. Key Objectives of Mentoring...................................... 154
Figure 16-3. The Roles of Influence and Choice 159
Figure 16-4. Intercultural Mentorship in Action............................. 160

SECTION 1
BASIC UNDERSTANDINGS

CHAPTER 1
Introduction

The background of this book

The seed idea for this book came through offering courses on leadership, discipleship and mentorship in the two doctoral programs at Western Seminary in the area of intercultural ministry/education for about two decades. The selection of textbooks and references in these three areas are mostly pragmatic and programmatic in focus, theologically weak and theoretically incoherent. It was brought to the front when a book of this scope and at this level could not be found. After prayers and consultations for a year, a writing plan emerged, leading to the formation of a team of three.

How this book came about

The three co-authors share the same theological conviction, theoretical orientation and ministerial motivation through decade-long association and partnership in the academic programs at Western Seminary. Under the guidance of the Holy Spirit, we met and worked together regularly for discussion and deliberation on campus. With mutual understanding and division of labor, we enjoyed the process of this book project together.

This book is one of the titles in the "Relational Paradigm Series of CDRR" at Western Seminary. It is a sequel to *Transformational Change in Christian Ministry* (2022) co-authored by Enoch Wan and Jon Raibley. Theoretically, this book is an integration of "relational realism paradigm," "relational transformational paradigm" and "relational interactionism paradigm" for practical ministries of intercultural leadership/discipleship/mentorship.

Background of the co-authors

Enoch Wan has served on the faculty at Western Seminary for twenty-one years, leading two doctoral programs in intercultural studies and intercultural education. He served for two terms as president of the Evangelical Missiological Society and as vice president in various capacities for two decades. Enoch began his research on the two paradigms (i.e., relational realism and diaspora missiology) during his sabbatical as scholar-in-residence at Yale Divinity School two decades ago. Since then, he has published many articles and dozens of books on these two themes.[1]

Mark Hedinger came to this book project after a long history of mission work and study. After living and working in Mexico for twelve years, Mark served in mid-level leadership of a mission agency. In those roles he became convinced of the importance of intercultural training for mission practitioners. After completing a doctorate at Western Seminary under the direction of Dr. Enoch Wan, he eventually joined a mission training program headquartered in Portland, Oregon. That organization, named CultureBound, offers training for intercultural ministry and second language acquisition to intercultural workers sent out from many different nations. Mark also continues to teach intercultural communication and education through Western Seminary and a number of other schools. The key idea that ties Mark together with the other authors of this work is a commitment to the relational perspective. All three authors are convinced that life and ministry are much more aligned with relationships than with methods and techniques. That idea is central to all elements of Mark's ministry, including this book.

Jon Raibley has been employed by Western Seminary since 1988, working with their distance education and online programs. He has travelled to the Philippines on two occasions, spending a total of eighteen months assisting church planters there. Under Enoch Wan's supervision, Jon completed Western's Doctor of Education in Intercultural Education program in 2021, and published an article on transformational learning.[2] His dissertation explored the experiences of online students with communities of learning.[3] The two then spent a year on the book project, leading to publication of this volume in 2022.

The purpose of this book

The purpose of this book is to provide an integrative understanding of transformational growth in terms of intercultural leadership, discipleship, and mentorship for Christian ministry.

---

[1] See Appendix 1 for a list of publications on the relational paradigm and the diaspora missiology paradigm.

[2] Enoch Wan and Jon Raibley, "Transforming Meaning Perspectives and Intercultural Education," in *Covenant Transformative Learning Theory and Practice for Mission* (Western Seminary Press, 2021), 147–62.

[3] Jon Raibley, "Experiencing Communities of Learning: A Phenomenological Study of Students Enrolled in Western Seminary's Online Master of Divinity Program" (Portland, Oregon, Western Seminary, 2021).

Definition of key terms

- **Christian Interculturality** – Believers from various cultures progressively increasing toward becoming of one mind (Phil. 2:2) under the sovereignty of the Father, the Lordship of Christ, and the guidance and power of the Holy Spirit. This process involves life interaction and the mutual pursuit of Scriptural truth, done in a spirit of love, unity, and humility.
- **Intercultural Leadership** – Patterned interaction across cultural boundaries between a leader and his/her followers whereby the process (of inspiration → initiative → implementation → influence), under the guidance and illumination of the Comforter (the HS), leads towards transformational change (i.e., scripturally sound, theologically supported and contextually relevant) individually and/or institutionally, instead of "transgressional change."
- **Intercultural Discipleship** –a 2-step process (within the context of the convergence between the Triune God and at least two distinct cultural groups) by which a non-Christian (a) firstly being born again by the Holy Spirit, then (b) becoming a faithful follower of Christ in total submission to His lordship as required by Christ and prescribed by the Scriptures, walking in the Holy Spirit (vertically) with fruitfulness, taking up his/her cross (denying himself/herself) and forsaking all (horizontally). (Mt 10:37-38; 16-24; Mk 8:34; Lk 14:26-27,33)
- **Intercultural Mentorship** –a reciprocal learning relationship in which the mentor and one or more mentees interact across cultural boundaries to influence each other to become more like Christ and better equipped to serve others. This process is dependent on the commitment of each member to grow in their vertical relationship with the Triune God.
- **Relational Realism Paradigm** – "Ontologically, "relational realism" is defined as "the systematic understanding that 'reality' is primarily based on the 'vertical relationship' between God and the created order and secondarily 'horizontal relationship' within the created order." Epistemologically, "relational realism" is to be defined as "the systematic understanding that God is the absolute Truth and the Perfect Knowledge, and only in relationship to HIM is there the possibility of human knowledge and understanding of truth and reality."[4]
- **Relational Interactionism** - is an interdisciplinary narrative framework that develops from practical considerations of dynamic interaction of

---

[4] Enoch Wan, "The Paradigm of 'Relational Realism'." Occasional Bulletin 19, no. 2 (Spring 2006), 1.

personal Beings/beings, forming realistic relational networks in multiple contexts (i.e., theo-culture, angel-culture and human-culture) and with various consequences.[5]

- **Relational Transformation Paradigm** — transformational change is to be understood within "relational realism paradigm."
- **Transformational Growth** – The dynamism and process of positive change, originated vertically from the Triune-God and ushered in the relational reality horizontally, through the process of interaction between personal Beings (the Triune God) and human beings (at micro and macro levels) multi-dimensionally, i.e. spiritual, moral, social, behavioral dimensions at personal and/or institutional levels – the opposite of transgressional change.[6]
- **Transgressional Decline** – Change caused by the dynamism from the enemy of the Triune God and by nature that is contrary to the attribute of God and His will, His revelation in Jesus Christ and the Scripture - the opposite is "transformational change." (Wan & Raibley 2022:7)
- **Relational Transformational Leadership** — the ability of a leader whose organizational vision and operational influence vertically received (from the Triune God and guided by the truth of the Scripture) then horizontally implemented can usher in transformational change at both individual and organizational levels.
- **Relational Transformational Discipleship** – a 2-step process (within the context of the convergence between the Triune God and the Christian community) by which a non-Christian (a) firstly being born again by the Holy Spirit, then (b) becoming a faithful follower of Christ in total submission to His lordship as required by Christ and prescribed by the Scriptures, walking in the Holy Spirit (vertically) with fruitfulness, taking up his/her cross (denying himself/herself) and forsaking all (horizontally). (Mt 10:37-38; 16-24; Mk 8:34; Lk 14:26-27,33)
- **Relational Transformational Mentorship** - a reciprocal learning relationship in which the mentor and one or more mentees interact across cultural boundaries to influence each other to become more like Christ and better equipped to serve others.

---

[5] Enoch Wan, "Rethinking Urban Mission in Terms of Spiritual and Social Transformational Change" (Missiological Society of Ghana/WAMS Biennial International Conference, Virtual, October 26, 2021).

[6] Enoch Wan, "Relational Transformational Leadership: An Asian Christian Perspective." Asian Missions Advance, April 2021:2-7.

The organization of the book

This book is built around the repeating theme of "Being-Belonging-Becoming" that was introduced in the recent volume, *Transformational Change in Christian Ministry.*[7]

That Being-Belonging-Becoming picture of human transformation is first introduced (Chapters 1 - 3), and then applied to the ministry of Leadership (chapters 4-7), Discipleship (Chapters 8-12) and Mentoring (chapters 13-17). The book ends with a concluding chapter (18).

---

[7] Enoch Wan and Jon Raibley, *Transformational Change in Christian Ministry*, Second Edition (Portland, Oregon: Western Academic Publishers, 2022).

CHAPTER 2
Theoretical Foundations of Relational Intercultural Transformation

Introduction

In this chapter, we will first deal with the definition and concept of "interculturality" then introduce theoretical foundations of relational intercultural transformation.

Inter-Disciplinarity

Jensenius addresses the matter of interdisciplinary approach in social sciences and provides the following diagram to help clarify the distinction and the progression in research in the figure below:

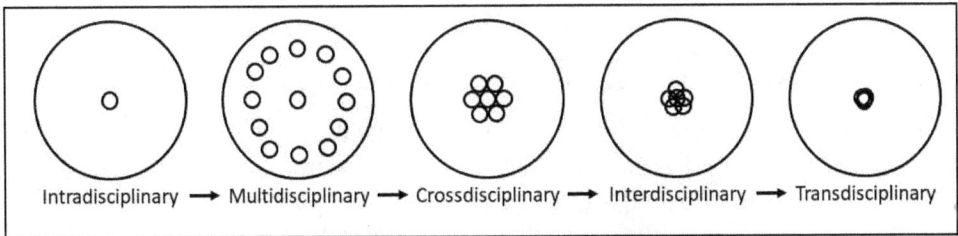

Figure 2-1. Distinction and Progression of Disciplinarities[8]

Marilyn Stember offers the following overview of different levels of disciplinarity:

- "Intradisciplinary: working within a single discipline.
- Multidisciplinary: people from different disciplines working together, each drawing on their disciplinary knowledge.
- Crossdisciplinary: viewing one discipline from the perspective of another.
- Interdisciplinary: integrating knowledge and methods from different disciplines, using a real synthesis of approaches.

---

[8] Alexander Refsum Jensenius, "Disciplinarities: Intra, Cross, Multi, Inter, Trans," *ARJ (English)* (blog), March 12, 2012, https://www.arj.no/2012/03/12/disciplinarities-2/.

- Transdisciplinary: creating a unity of intellectual frameworks beyond the disciplinary perspectives."[9]

Intercultural Studies and Interculturality

Within an intercultural context, "culture" can be conceptualized as "a homogeneous unit where members share similarity (i.e. in belief and behavior, attitude and action)," and "interculturality" as "the dynamics of interplay of cultural units (macro-level) or members of different cultural units interacting with one and other (micro-level)."[10] The combination of various prefixes for the word "cultural" will lead to the understanding of "interculturality" of various patterns as shown in the figure below:

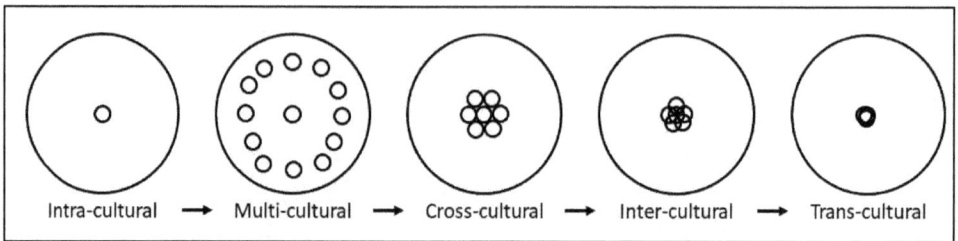

Intra-cultural ⟶ Multi-cultural ⟶ Cross-cultural ⟶ Inter-cultural ⟶ Trans-cultural

Figure 2-2. Distinction and Progression of "Interculturality"

There are five patterns of interculturality, if we do three things, (a) adapting the two figures above, (b) substituting the word 'disciplinary' with the word 'culture,' and (c) acknowledging the distinction and progression of the combination. The five cultural patterns can be described as follows:

- Intra-cultural: working within a single cultural unit.
- Multi-cultural: people from different cultural units coexisting together.
- Cross-cultural: viewing one cultural unit from the perspective of another.
- Inter-cultural: convergence of cultural units, members interacting and integrating.
- Trans-cultural: operating beyond one's own cultural unit by reaching out.

---

[9] Marilyn Stember, "Advancing the Social Sciences through the Interdisciplinary Enterprise," *The Social Science Journal* 28, no. 1 (1991): 1–14, DOI: 10.1016/0362-3319(91)90040-B.

[10] Enoch Wan and Natalie Kim, *Relational Intercultural Training for Practitioners of Business As Mission: Theory and Practice* (Western Academic Publishers, 2022), 29. The following diagram and list of cultural patterns are from this source as well.

In the remainder of this chapter, we will introduce some of the foundational theories behind transformational change. Enoch Wan has proposed various paradigms that describe the role of relationship in creation and change. The key frameworks are listed in the figure below, then each explained in more depth.

Framework	Key Elements
Relational Realism Paradigm	Reality exists and was created by the Triune God, who is eternally in relationship, and has built relationship into all of creation.
Relational Transformative Paradigm	Transformative change is a result of divine aid, plus godly input, plus positive response. Importance of vertical and horizontal interaction
Relational Interactionism Paradigm	Transformational vs. transgressional change. Being (who is interacting?), belonging (how are they interacting?), becoming (what influence to they have on each other?)
Relational Transformational Growth	Application of the three paradigms by intentionally interacting with others for positive influence

Figure 2-3. Relational Frameworks

Relational Realism paradigm

The key idea of the relational realism paradigm is that knowledge is best realized in the relational networks of God and the created order. In this sense, it is also the epistemological understand that "God is the absolute Truth and the Perfect Knowledge, and the only in relationship to Him is there the possibility of human knowledge and understanding of truth and reality."[11] In summary:

1   God is the most Real; only in relationship to Him does the created order exist.
2   God is the Absolute and Infinite who transcends time, space, and circumstance; whereas His created order is otherwise until in the "eschaton" when there will still be distinction between the Creator and the created order.
3   Human understanding is best comprehended and experienced in relational networks of God and the created order.

---

[11] Enoch Wan, "The Paradigm of 'Relational Realism,'" *Occasional Bulletin* 19, no. 2 (Spring 2006): 1.

4   Apart from relationship with God in terms of His enablement (common grace and general revelation) and enlightenment (special grace and special revelation), knowledge and human understanding is impossible and imperfect.[12]

Relational reality involves multiple dimensions, multiple levels and multiple contexts. These are outlined in the figure below.

[12] Wan, "The Paradigm of Relational Realism," 1–2.

ORDER/ SYSTEM			RELATIONSHIP (MULTI-DIMENSION, MULTI-LEVEL, MULTI-CONTEXT)	BIBLICAL REFERENCE
UNCREATED ORDER – TRIUNE GOD		Essence	Intra-Trinitarian relationship of Father, Son & Holy Spirit, with perfect unity & harmony	John 17; Phil. 2:1-11
		Nature	Absolute, transcendent, infinite	
CREATED ORDER	Angel	Essence	Created and ruled by God	Heb. 1:14, 2:6-8, 16
		Nature	• Not absolute, perfect, infinite • Superior to humanity & nature • Since the Fall - disharmony	
	Human	Essence	• Willed to existence by God ("let us...") • Created with God's breath & image is both male & female; reaffirmed after fall and flood • Designated by God with authority to rule & subdue, provided with good • Blessed by God to be fruitful & multiply	Gen. 1:26-30, 2:7-9, 5:1-2; 9:1-7; Ps. 8; Heb. 2; Eph. 2:11-22
		Nature	• Strife, conflict, disharmony since the Fall • Within the redeemed humanity: Reconciled and mediated by Christ with unity restored and harmony obtained	
	Nature	Essence	• Created and sustained by God • Cursed after the fall • In Christ, restored by/for/through Him	Acts 17:26; Eph. 2:1-14; Col. 1:16-18
		Nature	• Harmony before the fall • Cursed; groans for redemption • "Shalom" ushering in by the messianic rule of Christ	

Figure 2-4. Multi-level, Multi-dimension, Multi-stage of Relationship[13]

Relational Transformational Paradigm

Relational realism claims that reality exists, and that it is created by a Triune God who is eternally relational and has built relationships into the nature of

---

[13] Adapted from Wan, The Paradigm of Relational Realism, 3.

creation. The *relational transformational paradigm* builds on relational realism by showing how change and growth occurs. It states that transformative change is a result of divine aid, plus godly input, plus positive response. A person who is willing to grow can experience positive change through vertical and horizontal interactions, in the context of a relational community.[14] This process can be illustrated as in the following figure.

Divine Aid
+ **Godly leader's influence**
+ **Follower's positive response**
+ **Interaction of a faith community**
= **Transformational Change**

Figure 2-5. Transformational Change Equation[15]

A theology of Gospel transformation begins with transformational change (2 Cor. 3:18, 5:17; Acts 3:19; Gal 5:22-23; Ro 12:2; Phil 1:6; Lk 6:43-45; Col 3:5) of an individual believer then extend to his/her network of relationships in multiple contexts of marriage, family, workplace and community. The essence of the relational transformational paradigm is illustrated in the figure below.

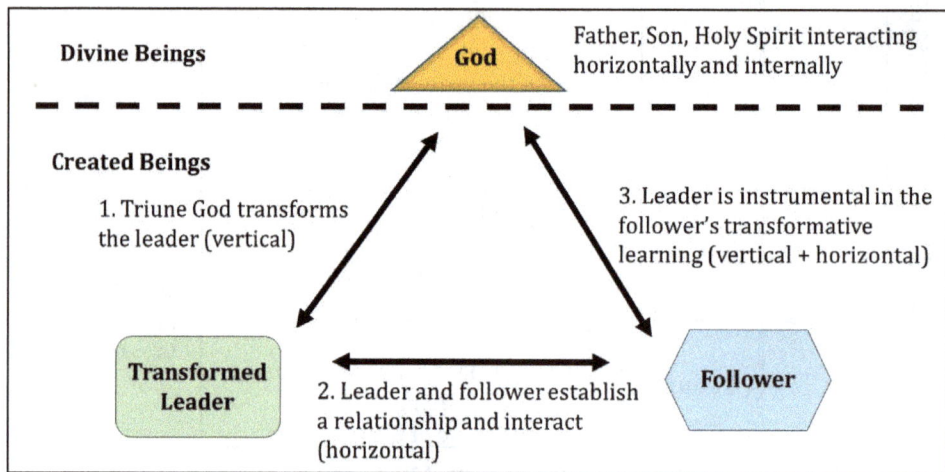

Figure 2-6. The Process of Transformational Growth

---

[14] Enoch Wan and Mark Hedinger, "Transformative Ministry for the Majority World Context; Applying Relational Approaches," *Occasional Bulletin* 31, no. 2 (Spring 2018): 7.

[15] Enoch Wan, "Relational Intercultural Leadership and Mentorship" (Unpublished material, February 14, 2022), 5.

Various types of interaction occur in the process of transformational change. Vertical interaction occurs as God transforms the leader and the follower. This process includes God saving them by the power of the Father's choosing, the atonement of the Son, and the regeneration and empowering of the Spirit. The leader and follower in return submit to the will of the Father, the Lordship of the Son, and the leading of the Spirit. At the same time, they participate in horizontal interactions with each other and others, demonstrating internal transformation through their words and actions (2 Thessalonians 2:17).

As the leader and follower both experience transformation through their vertical relationships with God, this growth should be reflected in and encouraged by horizontal relationships within faith communities. By God's grace and provision, these relationship mirror, although imperfectly, the Trinity's perfect unity and harmony. The relationship between leader and follower will be one of these horizontal connections which give opportunities for both to intentionally choose to grow in godliness and unity.

The relational transformative paradigm maintains that horizontal relationships are transformative, but only because that transformation is directed and empowered by the Triune God. Jack Mezirow correctly sees human relationship and dialog as fundamental to the process of change and transformation[16], but the relational transformational paradigm sees two additional points as essential:

- The Trinity is the source of the dynamic power for transformation. The Father is the "Fount of blessing" and "source of wisdom" (James 1:5-18), Jesus Christ, the Son, is our Savior and Lord (Col 1:15-20), and the Holy Spirit provides of regeneration, illumination, direction, and power (Titus 3:5, 2 Timothy 3:16, John 16:13-14).
- The faith community is essential in the transformation process. "It is not simply a series of one-on-one relationships that foster transformation. Interaction with the larger group – the Church, local congregations and the faith community of Christians – is also key to transformation; especially to the cyclical multiplication of leaders."[17] It is important to have "*koinonia* and *ecclesia*" – Christian fellowship and congregation.

Relational Interactionism Paradigm

The *relational interactionism paradigm* takes a closer look at the process of transformation by exploring the interactions that take place between *beings*, in

---

[16] Jack Mezirow, ed. *Learning as Transformation: Critical Perspectives on a Theory in Progress.* 1st edition (San Francisco, CA: Jossey-Bass, 2000).

[17] Wan and Hedinger, "Transformative Ministry for the Majority World Context," 7.

the context of *belonging*, and with the result of *becoming* new beings with new behavior. The following figure describes this process.

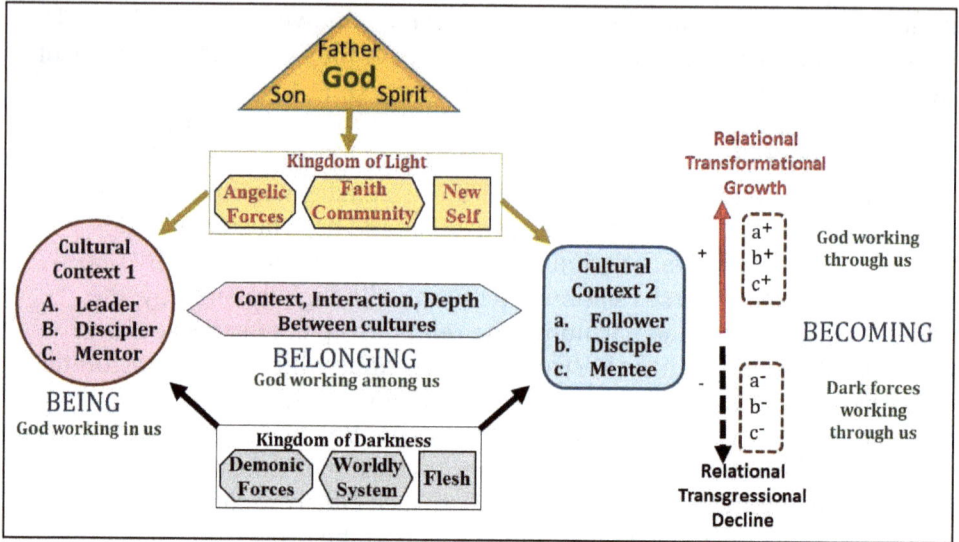

Figure 2-7. Relational Intercultural Transformational Change

Robert Hinde defines relationship as "a series of interactions between individuals who know each other such that each interaction can be influenced by past interactions and by expectations of interactions in the future."[18]Based on this definition, Enoch Wan and Natalie Kim identify five key components of relationship. They state, "the *people* who are involved in *interactions* in the *context* where they know each other at a *different level* and the interactions *influence* the way they interact in the future."[19] These components are described in the figure below.

---

[18] Robert A. Hinde, *Relationships: A Dialectical Perspective* (London, U.K.: Psychology Press, 1997), 48.

[19] Wan and Kim, *Relational Intercultural Training for Practitioners of Business As Mission*, 75.

Component	Description
Being(s)/ being(s)	The individuals, both divine and of the created order, who are involved in the interaction.
Interaction	The act of making connections and relating to one another.
Context	The setting of the interaction, including location, time, space/ distance, and cultural identities
Depth	The closeness of a relationship, based on one's knowledge of the other person, consistency or frequency of their interactions, and the context that exists between them.
Influence	The way in which one person affects another. Influence may vary in strength and direction over time, encouraging the other to become more Christ-like, or less.

Figure 2-8. Components of Relationship[20]

Being

The story, character, and actions of the individuals involved in a relationship have a large impact on their connection, their interactions, and the reciprocal influence they have on each other.

A person's story is the role they play in God's overarching history of his created order. It includes such things as family influence, cultural identification, personality traits, gifting, experiences, roles, and needs. These combine to affect how people see themselves, and how they interact with others.

That person's character both influences their story, and is shaped by it. Character involves the values, assumptions, and beliefs that they learned from their childhood culture, and that they've adopted in their subsequent journey through life. Paul Hiebert and Eloise Meneses include these in their description of worldview. They state, "People in a society share symbols, beliefs, feelings, and values. Beneath these are the basic categories and assumptions people make about the nature of things and the logic that relates these to form a coherent understanding of reality. These basic assumptions about the nature of reality form what we call the people's worldview."[21] These worldviews are "largely unnamed, unexamined, and unassailable. It is particularly difficult to examine our own worldview because it is hard to think about what we are thinking with."[22] Hiebert also describes how worldviews interact with values and beliefs: "...worldview serves as the foundation on which people construct

---

[20] Adapted from Wan and Kim, *Relational Intercultural Training*, 76–78.

[21] Paul G. Hiebert and Eloise Hiebert Meneses, *Incarnational Ministry: Planting Churches in Band, Tribal, Peasant, and Urban Societies* (Grand Rapids: Baker Books, 1995), 41.

[22] Hiebert and Meneses, 320.

17

their explicit belief and value systems, and the social institutions in which they live their daily lives. Most people take their worldview for granted and those who challenge it are seen not as wrong but as crazy!"[23] Worldviews produce value systems; values, in turn, "affect our behavior, driving us to do things in ways that reflect kingdom priorities."[24]

Character includes the identities that people see themselves as having, and the various levels of formation they've experienced, including integrity, morality, and developmental, social, and spiritual formation. Character is demonstrated by what the person does, which includes the following activities. In addition, these activities influence one's character.

- Feeling, attitudes (affective)
- Thinking: thinking process and knowledge (cognitive)
- Choosing. Thinking and feeling leading to doing (volitional)
- Actions: patterns of conduct (behavioral)

Belonging

The sense of belonging within a relationship is affected by the interactions that take place between the people involved. The context of the interactions, their frequency, content, and tone, and the depth or transparency of the conversations all help determine how much a person feels a part of the group, and how much reciprocal influence takes place because of the relationships between group members.

Interaction involves "a process of interaction and involvement, so that two people of different cultural backgrounds may develop personal relationships by transferring their unfamiliar interaction into a familiar and normal experience."[25] Stephen and Mary Lowe state, "The more connected we are to one another through reciprocal interactions, the greater the likelihood for continued growth and development of the whole person."[26]

Wang and Kim discuss the power of relationships to result in either transformative or transgressional change:

Relationships are evaluative and have infinite potential for growth and improvement. Good relationships produce trust, fairness, mutuality,

---

[23] Paul G. Hiebert, "Conversion and Worldview Transformation," *International Journal of Frontier Missions* 14, no. 2 (June 1997): 85.

[24] James Lawrence, *Growing Leaders: Cultivating Discipleship for Yourself and Others* (Peabody, MA: Hendrickson Publishers, Inc., 2004), 245.

[25] Adapted from Wan and Kim, *Relational Intercultural Training*, 77.

[26] Stephen D. Lowe and Mary E. Lowe, "Spiritual Formation in Theological Distance Education: An Ecosystems Model," *Christian Education Journal*, 3, 7 (2010): 127.

encouragement, joy, respect, and beauty. However, people who struggle in relationships such as in families, workplaces, or ministries can experience miscommunication, lack of trust, conflict, exhaustion, disengagement, hostile atmosphere, and constant judgment toward one another.[27]

Becoming

People who interact together influence each other to change. This change can either be positive, leading a person to become more like Christ, or negative, pulling them further from closeness and obedience to God. We have called these two opposing types of change 'transformational growth' and 'transgressional decline.'

Lowe and Lowe list six areas of human wholeness: physical, intellectual, emotional, social, moral, and spiritual aspects.[28] They state that the New Testament's "one another" commands are all represented by these six dimensions. Their list is shown in the following figure.

Elements of Human Wholeness	"One Another" Commands
Spiritual	Confess your sins to one another; pray for one another; build up one another; forgive one another; love one another; submit to one another
Moral	Do not lie to one another; do not slander one another; do not judge one another; honor one another
Social	Accept one another; bear one another's burdens; forbear one another; be at peace with one another; live in harmony with one another; be hospitable to one another
Emotional	Be kind to one another; be devoted to one another; encourage one another; show concern for one another; comfort one another
Intellectual	Teach one another; speak to one another; stimulate one another; admonish one another
Physical	Wash one another's feet; greet one another with a holy kiss, wait for one another

Figure 2-9. New Testament "One Another" Commands and Developmental Dimensions[29]

This movement toward Christ-likeness is influenced by the relationships that we are involved in. Those influences can be positive or negative, but we also have a choice in how we respond to those influences, as shown in the following figure.

---

27 Wan and Kim, *Relational Intercultural Training for Practitioners of Business As Mission*, 78.
28 Lowe and Lowe, *Ecologies of Faith in a Digital Age*, 184–85.
29 Adapted from Lowe and Lowe, *Ecologies of Faith in a Digital Age*, 185.

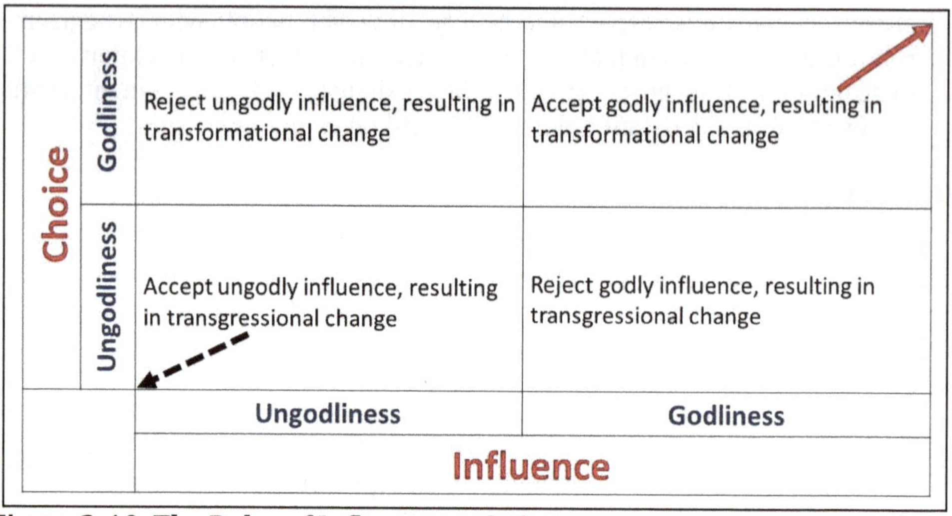

Figure 2-10. The Roles of Influence and Choice

Relational Transformational Growth

Relational interactionism describes the process of change, but does not dictate whether that change is positive or negative. Relational Transformational Growth focuses on those interactions that produce positive change, making a Christian more conformed to the image of Christ (Romans 8:29).

This transformational growth is not a naïve belief that becoming a follower of Christ automatically resolves all problems in a person's life. Rather, Paul witnessed this type of growth in the lives of believers in Thessalonica. He states, "We remember before our God and Father your work produced by faith, your labor prompted by love, and your endurance inspired by hope in our Lord Jesus Christ" (1 Thess. 1:3). Transformational growth is based on the reality of a glorious and gracious God "who works in you to will and to act in order to fulfill his good purpose" (Phil. 2:13).

Figure 2-11 lists some examples of transformational growth, contrasted with examples of transgressional decline.

Examples Domain	Transgressional (Conformed to World)	Transformational (Renewing of Your Mind)
Cognitive	Harmful stereotypes and thinking patterns	Faith, transformed mind, right thinking
Affective	Prejudice, pride, fear	Humility, trust, unity
Behavioral	Discrimination, injustice	Love, Service

Figure 2-11. Examples of Transgressional and Transformational Changes Within the Learning Domains

Summary

In this chapter, we have explored the theoretical frameworks of interculturality and relational transformational growth with its supporting paradigms. In the following chapter we will take a deeper look at how these theoretical understandings can function together in intercultural ministry contexts. In Sections 2 through 4, we will examine that functionality in depth for ministry in terms of leadership, discipleship, and mentoring.

Summary

CHAPTER 3
Thematic Understanding of Intercultural Transformational Growth

Theories of Intercultural Learning

Intercultural learning theories fall into two large classes:

First, theories that support interculturalism per se. These theories are interested in encouraging interculturalism, reducing ethnocentrism, combatting prejudice and promoting solidarity of people across a plurality of cultural identities. Authors from this perspective would include Milton Bennett[30].

These theories are not so much interested in helping a given person live and work well outside of his/her home culture. They are more interested in developing a positive relationship of all people to all other people along with a decrease in unhealthy attitudes such as prejudice and stereotyping.

A second approach to intercultural learning is demonstrated by such authors as Lingenfelter,[31] Plueddemann,[32] Ott,[33] and Shaw[34]. These Christian authors approach the idea of intercultural learning from the perspective of equipping people for the task of moving outside of their home culture, entering into another culture, and taking up life and ministry in that new cultural milieu. While issues of appropriate attitudes and avoidance of prejudice are certainly of high importance, this school of thought also focuses on skills, attitudes, and knowledge that will help facilitate positive outcomes.

Within this second class of intercultural learning theories we find numerous references to educational theory in general and to intercultural theory in particular. These approaches seek to facilitate student learning by understanding the nature of the student and creating an appropriate mixture of

---

[30] Milton J. Bennett, "Towards Ethnorelativism: A Developmental Model of Intercultural Sensitivity," in *Education for the Intercultural Experience* (Yarmouth, ME: Intercultural Press, Inc., 1993), 21–71.

[31] Judith E. Lingenfelter and Sherwood G. Lingenfelter, *Teaching Cross-Culturally: An Incarnational Model for Learning and Teaching* (Grand Rapids: Baker Academic, 2003).

[32] James E. Plueddemann, *Leading Across Cultures: Effective Ministry and Mission in the Global Church* (Downers Grove, IL: IVP Academic, 2009).

[33] Craig Ott, *Teaching and Learning across Cultures: A Guide to Theory and Practice* (Grand Rapids, MI: Baker Academic, 2021).

[34] Perry Shaw, *Transforming Theological Education: A Practical Handbook for Integrative Learning* (Carlisle, Cumbria UK: Langham Partnership, 2014).

concrete experience, reflective observation, abstract conceptualizing and active experimentation.[35]

Cultural distinctions like power distance, individualism/collectivism,[36] universalism/particularism[37] are likewise part of this model, encouraging the intercultural educator to at least be aware, and hopefully be skillful, at navigating cultural variations.

Craig Ott discusses five key dimensions that affect intercultural teaching and intercultural learning: cognitive patterns of the people involved, worldview, social relationships that the people have experienced, the media preferences of groups, and the environment.[38]

The challenge for educators is to simultaneously work in horizontal and vertical relational dimensions. It is easy to focus on the horizontal issues of methods, student recruitment, or cultural learning styles without factoring active Divine involvement into our understanding of the educational process.

In that light, Robert Pazmiño offers a very appropriate correction, for instance in his 1997 work, *Foundational Issues in Christian Education*. He says, "An effective curriculum weds Christian content and experience and thereby is potentially life transforming. This potential requires the active and receptive participation of persons who seek to learn and are open to God's instruction as mediated through human teachers."[39]

The Transformational Learning approach that we will present in this book will consider God to be actively involved and simultaneously see human beings as responsible to develop educational contexts where learning happens as people move from their native "being" into a "becoming" that is influenced by the relationships that surround them (belonging). The first "belonging" relationship is between a person and Triune God. We will develop this simultaneously vertical and horizontal model of intercultural learning more fully in the pages to come.

---

[35] Alice Y. Kolb and David A. Kolb, "The Kolb Learning Style Inventory Version 3.1: 2005 Technical Specifications" (Hay Resources Direct, 2005).

[36] Geert Hofstede, "The 6 Dimensions Model of National Culture," Geert Hofstede, accessed February 1, 2023, https://geerthofstede.com/culture-geert-hofstede-gert-jan-hofstede/6d-model-of-national-culture/.

[37] Fons Trompenaars and Charles Hampden-Turner, *Riding the Waves of Culture: Understanding Diversity in Global Business*, Third edition (New York: McGraw-Hill, 2012).

[38] Ott, *Teaching and Learning across Culture*.

[39] Robert W. Pazmiño, *Foundational Issues in Christian Education: An Introduction in Evangelical Perspective*, 3rd edition (Grand Rapids, MI: Baker Academic, 2008), 225. See also Robert W. Pazmiño, *God Our Teacher: Theological Basics in Christian Education* (Eugene, OR: Wipf and Stock, 2016).

Interculturality

Christian Interculturality – Believers from various cultures progressively increasing toward becoming of one mind (Phil. 2:2) under the sovereignty of the Father, the Lordship of Christ, and the guidance and power of the Holy Spirit. This process involves life interaction and the mutual pursuit of Scriptural truth, done in a spirit of love, unity, and humility.

Intercultural ministry from a relational transformational perspective is the formal/informal/non-formal process by which a believer interacts relationally with others in order to develop and enrich both their "being" and their "doing" in multidimensional ways (such as cognitive, affective, volitional, behavioral, etc.) within a cross-cultural context.[40] Foundational assumptions for this definition include those listed in the figure below.

Category	Description
Ontological	Ministry is done within the context of personal beings/ Beings. The best way of ministering is through relational interaction.
Epistemological	Subjective and objective dimensions of knowing are critically different, yet both should be included
Theoretical	A relational perspective is preferred over other perspectives, such as rationalistic, behavioral, communicative, and pragmatic. Directed toward positive (transformative) change.
Existential	"Doing" is not to be separated from "being" for there is a dynamic interplay and intricate relationship between the two.

Figure 3-1. Assumptions in Relational Intercultural Ministry[41]

Theories of Transformational Learning

Covenant Transformative Learning Theory

Transformative learning, also called transformational learning, was developed by Jack Mezirow in 1978. Enoch Wan and Ryan Gimple state,

Transformative learning theory describes worldview transformation through the language of meaning perspective transformation. Worldview

---

[40] Adapted from Enoch Wan, "A Theological Reflection on Inter-Cultural Reality and Intercultural Education" (Unpublished material, Portland, OR, 2020), 6.

[41] Adapted from Wan, "A Theological Reflection," 6.

refers to the central core assumptions shared by a community from which we perceive, reason, feel, and experience the world. Meaning perspectives are habits of mind and the interlayered connections of meaning schemes which form a worldview.[42]

They explain meaning perspectives further as "not only an organization of our cognitive structures, but they are the means by which we experience and relate to the world."[43]

Mezirow states, "I believe an act of learning can be called transformative only if it involves a fundamental questioning and reordering of how one thinks or acts."[44] He clarifies that this process of perspective transformation is one of "becoming critically aware of how we perceive, understand, and feel about our world; of reformulating these assumptions to permit a more inclusive, discriminating, permeable, and integrative perspective; and of making decisions or otherwise acting upon these new understandings."[45] In his view, this transformation takes place through discourse that assesses one's beliefs, feelings, and values, then forms a mental model of the person who is offering his or her perspective, reaches an understanding of that perspective, and chooses whether or not to adopt it as their own.[46]

This discourse, or interaction, is an important element of transformative learning theory. Mezirow states that true discourse takes place best in cultural systems that value "freedom, equality, tolerance, social justice, and rationality... safety, health, economic security, education, and emotional intelligence."[47] In intercultural settings, this interaction can be especially beneficial, as it can include insights from very different perspectives of the world and reality.

Wan and Gimple propose "covenant transformative learning theory" as a means of interacting with both Mezirow's transformative learning framework, and Esther Meek's "covenant epistemology." Meek argues against "modern and postmodern dichotomies leading to relativism or absolutism. Meek instead views (and experiences) knowing as the covenant response of a servant to her

---

[42] Ryan Gimple and Enoch Wan, *Covenant Transformative Learning: Theory and Practice* (Portland, Oregon: Western Seminary Press, 2021), 3.

[43] Gimple and Wan, *Covenant Transformative Learning*, 7.

[44] Stephen D. Brookfield, "Transformative Learning as Ideology Critique," in *Learning as Transformation: Critical Perspectives on a Theory in Progress* (San Francisco: Jossey-Bass, 2000), 139.

[45] Jack Mezirow, "A Guide to Transformative and Emancipatory Learning," 3.

[46] Jack Mezirow, "Transformative Learning as Discourse," *Journal of Transformative Education* 1, no. 1 (January 2003): 59–60.

[47] Jack Mezirow, "Learning to Think Like an Adult: Core Concepts of Transformation Theory," in *Learning as Transformation: Critical Perspectives on a Theory in Progress* (San Francisco: Jossey-Bass, 2000), 82.

Lord's overtures."[48] Similar to relational realism, covenant epistemology views reality as rooted in relationship. Meek states, "Covenant epistemology offers a developed account of and rationale for viewing knowing as relationally interpersoned."[49] She maintains that knowing should be a process that brings healing: "Knowing was meant to be therapeutic. The act ought to bring shalom, not just to the knower, but also to the known."[50] Wan and Gimple summarize how transformation occurs in covenant transformative learning theory:

1   "Encountering a reality that does not conform to our meaning perspectives may instigate a disorienting dilemma that begins the process of meaning perspective change.
2   When one meaning perspective changes, its interrelationship with other meaning perspectives may lead to changes in these interrelated meaning perspectives.
3   When several interwoven meaning perspectives transform, we experience worldview transformation.
4   This worldview transformation affects not just our beliefs, but also how we assign meaning, our expectations, and perceptions. As our meaning perspectives change, our expressed beliefs, feelings, and behaviors follow suit in time.

Covenant transformative learning theory affirms that worldviews are made up of sets of overlapping and interwoven meaning perspectives. Worldview transformation occurs as these sets of meaning perspectives are transformed. "[51]

---

[48] Gimple and Wan, *Covenant Transformative Learning*, 23.

[49] Esther Lightcap Meek, *Loving to Know: Introducing Covenant Epistemology* (Eugene, OR: Cascade Books, 2011), 49.

[50] Meek, *Loving to Know*, 51.

[51] Gimple and Wan, *Covenant Transformative Learning*, 83. We have divided their description into a numbered list to show the sequential nature of the process they describe.

Theories of Intercultural Education and Relational Pedagogy

Approach	Definition
Teaching as transformation (Knight, p. 99)	A process of transformation in which teachers are generators of knowledge within the daily uncertainty of the classroom experience. The teacher must be a person who is able to respond within the context of ever-changing settings. Thus teacher training needs to produce "teacher thinkers" rather than "technicists."
Relational Pedagogy (Relational Being, p. 250)	The dialogic classroom Expanding participation to include all students, while preventing a few opinionated or articulate students from dominating discussion Reducing control over the direction of discussion, so that student concerns more easily determine the topics Crediting students with intelligibility as opposed to correcting them Replacing the goal of Truth with that of expanding the range of intelligible realities
Cognitive Apprenticeship (Vygotsky's views on development) p. 251-255	The teacher must share not only his or her knowledge of content with the student, but the heuristics (or know-how) vital to using such knowledge in practice
Liberation/Empowerment (Freire)	Education should foster a critical consciousness ("conscientization") Practices that bring people together and enable them to engage in collective action for the collective good
Facilitation/Coaching	Teaching as facilitator of student development, or a coach
Teaching is friendship	Traditional relationship between teacher and student is limited Multiples roles (like family relationships – nurturing, informing, facilitating, commiserating, etc.)

Figure 3-2. Approaches to Relational Intercultural Education[52]

Multi-level Relational Approaches to Ministry

The core concept for communicating between people is that there be some level of interaction or involvement. The following four figures show communication patterns in the following relational connections:

---

[52] Enoch Wan, "Issues and Practice Related to Intercultural Education: IE701 Lecture PowerPoint Notes," March 2021, 6–7.

- Figure 3-3: Within the Trinity
- Figure 3-4: Between humans and the creator
- Figure 3-5: Within a monocultural context
- Figure 3-6: Within an intercultural context

Area	Horizontal Communication Within the Trinity
Type of communication	Eternally interactive
Depth of interaction	Infinite
Change and transformation	God is the same today, tomorrow, forever

Figure 3-3. Communication Patterns: The Trinity

Area	Vertical communication between Creator and people
Type of communication	Common involvement through prayer, Bible, ministry of Holy Spirit. Occasional miracles of revelation – voices from heaven or animals speaking.
Depth of interaction	The Spirit teaches the deep things of God People grow (2 Peter 3:18) so communication is given when appropriate
Change and transformation	As powerful as being born again Grow in the grace and knowledge of the Lord Jesus Christ (2 Pet. 3:18)

Figure 3-4. Communication Patterns: Creator and People

Area	Horizontal communication within a single culture
Type of communication	Speech, music, education, etc. All of the forms of communication that a group has available, God can be involved by opening people's minds and hearts within their home culture and language.
Depth of interaction	Social norms speak to this. In some cultures, deep sharing of emotions, thoughts, and dreams. In other cultures, very limited communication.
Change and transformation	People lead and share with one another but God gives the transformation. Acts 16:14 example of horizontal and vertical communication together.

Figure 3-5. Communication Patterns in Monocultural Contexts

Area	Horizontal communication across cultural boundaries
Type of communication	Speech, music, education practiced by people of one culture with intent of reaching another culture. Miraculous possibilities as in speaking in tongues (Acts 2).
Depth of interaction	Begins superficial. With time and commitment, may grow deep. Requires growth of shared understanding.
Change and transformation	People lead and share with one another but God gives the transformation. Acts 16:14 example of horizontal and vertical communication together.

Figure 3-6. Communication Patterns in Intercultural Contexts

Relational Transformational Change and Intercultural Transformational Growth

Noel Chiu proposes the picture of an umbrella to illustrate the need to incorporate vertical and horizontal relationships. She states, "From a Christian perspective, an education model should not only take into account embracing diversity or finding dynamic and connection between differences, but there must also be a vertical link to the Creator which unifies people of different cultures and ethnicities."[53]

---

[53] Ai Chen (Noel) Chiu, "Key Parameters of Establishing Frontline LGBTQ Outreach" (Doctor of Education, Portland, Oregon, Western Seminary, 2021), 175.

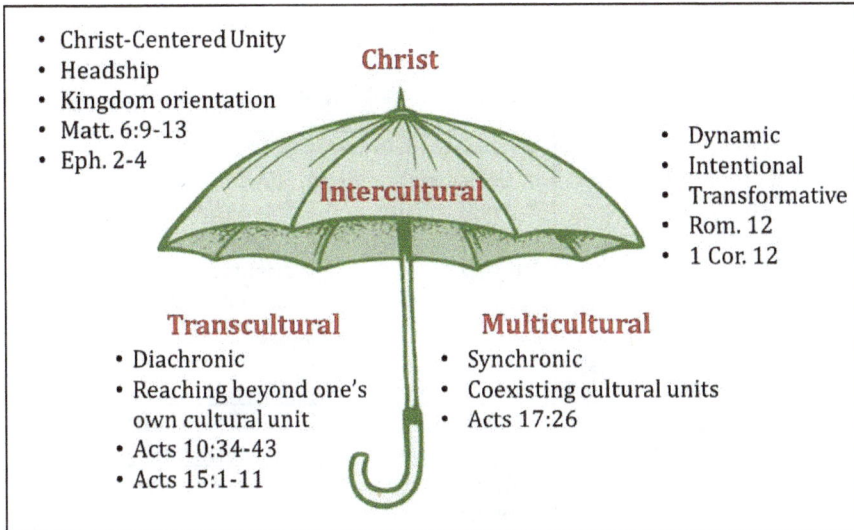

- Christ-Centered Unity
- Headship
- Kingdom orientation
- Matt. 6:9-13
- Eph. 2-4

Christ

Intercultural

- Dynamic
- Intentional
- Transformative
- Rom. 12
- 1 Cor. 12

Transcultural
- Diachronic
- Reaching beyond one's own cultural unit
- Acts 10:34-43
- Acts 15:1-11

Multicultural
- Synchronic
- Coexisting cultural units
- Acts 17:26

Figure 3-7. The Umbrella Model: Christ-Centered Unity[54]

She states,

> The umbrella illustration seeks to center all cultures and ethnicities toward a Christ-centered unity, and under this ultimate reality and focus, the vertical relationship between Beings and beings is the vertical drive which transforms different cultures toward the Kingdom culture, and the horizontal relationship between beings is the dynamic which helps different cultures and ethnic groups interact... Therefore, in the umbrella illustration, multiculturalism is no longer limited to acknowledging differences, but there is an underlying purpose for the diversity, and transculturalism is no longer direction-free transition and connection between different cultural and ethnic groups, but it is transformation with one ultimate vertical goal.

---

[54] Adapted from Chiu, *Key Parameters of Establishing Frontline LGBTQ Outreach,* 175.

Together, transcultural and multicultural approaches are covered under the intercultural umbrella, with a pinned focal point on top, which is Christ.[55]

Dimension	Transformative Change		
	Faith	**Love**	**Hope**
Vertical (God working in us)	1. Receptive of God's Word & work: salvation & illumination 2. Gain understanding of major themes, genres, & teachings of the Bible	1. Loyal to lordship of Christ as disciple 2. Abide in Him, passion for Him & His will	1. The fruit of the Spirit & walk in the Spirit (Gal. 4) 2. Kingdom-orientation & eternal perspective
	Cognitive: Knowing	**Attitudinal: Willing**	**Practical: Doing**
Horizontal (God working through us)	1. Practice God's truth in lifestyle and servanthood. 2. Member of faith-community: Koinonia & ecclesia	1. Channeling the love of God to others; mutuality & reciprocity, allelon "one and other" 2. Practice the Great Commandment & fulfill the Great Commission	1. Successfully attend and participate in church and its ministries 2. Exercise spiritual gifts to serve others 3. Be an agent of transformative change

Figure 3-8. Relational Training for Transformative Change: Dimensions & Aspects[56]

Level	Knowledge	Attitude	Skills
Personal (individual)	**Knowing:** Culture differences, barriers and bridges	**Willing:** Free from self-centeredness & ready to reach out	**Doing:** Competence to evangelize & serve others
Group (institutional)	Appreciative understanding of one another	Mutuality with respect & reciprocity	Godly partnership & God-glorifying reciprocity

Figure 3-9. Program Outcomes of Training for Transformational Change[57]

---

[55] Chiu, *Key Parameters of Establishing Frontline LGBTQ Outreach*, 176.

[56] Enoch Wan and Howard Chen, *Marketplace Transformation: Motivating and Mobilizing Chinese Churches in the Silicon Valley for Gospel Transformation.* (Portland, Oregon: Western Press, 2021), 19.

[57] Wan and Chen, 19.

Summary

In this section, we have introduced transformational growth, and looked at the theoretical frameworks of reality, relationships, transformation, and intercultural ministry. In the following sections, we will look at three overlapping approaches to serving God and people that combine these theories in connected and unique ways. As you think with us through intercultural ministry in the areas of leading, discipling, and mentoring, we invite you to explore how God can use those relationships to transform you and those around you to become more like Christ.

SECTION 2

TRANSFORMATIONAL GROWTH: INTERCULTURAL LEADERSHIP

The purpose of section 3 of this book is to briefly introduce and explain the "what," and "how" of transformational growth in intercultural leadership. There are three chapters in Section 3 sequentially dealing with one of the three phases of the transformational process: being, belonging, and becoming.

Chapter 4 provides introductory discussion on relational and transformational leadership, in comparison to the popular view on leadership. According to Figure 2-7, the remaining chapters of this section are organized as follows:

- Chapter 5 – "being" in the practice of intercultural leadership (OR "who all are interacting?")
- Chapter 6 – "belonging" in the practice of intercultural leadership (OR "how are they interacting?")
- Chapter 7 – "becoming" in the practice of intercultural leadership (OR what influence do they have on each other and beyond, leading to transformational growth?")

CHAPTER 4
Intercultural Leadership Introduction

Introduction

This chapter is introductory to section 3 on intercultural leadership, integrating the theory of relational interactionism and the paradigm of transformational change for growth.

Purpose of the chapter

The purpose of section 3 of this book is to briefly introduce and explain the "what," and "how" to practice relational intercultural leadership. Chapter 4 is an introductory chapter on the topic for section 3. For the sake of clarity, several key terms are defined below.

Definition of Key Terms

- **Leadership** — Patterned interaction between a leader and his/her followers whereby the process (of inspiration → initiative → implementation → influence), under the guidance and illumination of the Comforter (the HS), leads toward transformational change (i.e., scripturally sound, theologically supported and contextually relevant) individually and/or institutionally, instead of "transgressional change."
- **Relational Intercultural Leadership** — The godly influence of a genuine "follower of Christ" on the follower(s), based on his vertical connection with the Triune God (i.e., the sovereignty of the Father, the Lordship of Christ and unity in the Spirit) and godly interaction with fellow Kingdom laborers horizontally with transformational change holistically within an intercultural context.
- **Relational Transformational Leadership** — the ability of a leader whose organizational vision and operational influence vertically received (from the Triune God and guided by the truth of the Scripture) then horizontally implemented can usher in transformational change at both individual and organizational levels.
- **Narrative Framework:** A story-based structure for describing a person's understanding of and approach to life. Narrative framework includes both macro and micro views of history. The macro view is God's eternal meta-narrative, centered around Christ and his redemptive

relationship with creation.[58] The micro view describes a person's individual story within that metanarrative, combining one's experiences and self-identity with their worldview, including their foundational assumptions, values, and beliefs.[59]

- **Relational Transformational Growth**: The process of "becoming" in the children of God (with *imago Christi*), brought about by the Spirit of God through the Word of God in the context of the faith community (*koinonia* and *ecclesia*) of God to the glory of God based on the *missio-Dei* of the Triune God.[60]
  - **Personal Transformation** (being – ontological change): God working in us towards being Christ-like and Spirit-led, breaking loose from autonomous operation (idiosyncratic and narcissistic style) and leading to change and growth (*imago-Dei* → *imago Christo*) in three phases: being, belonging, and becoming.
  - **Social Transformation** (being → belonging[61] → becoming): God working through an aggregate of transformed Christians (at both individual and institutional levels) spiritually (saving souls) and socially (ushering in *shalom*) for redemption, reconciliation, and transformation[62] in a process of three phases: being, belonging, and becoming.
  - **Spiritual Transformation** (being→belonging→becoming): God working in us, working among us, and working through us for the fulfillment of His will to grow and to glorify Him.

A Narrative Study of the Transgressive Leadership of Satan and the Transformative Leadership of Jesus Christ

Transgressive Leadership of Satan

Though created innocent and living in a perfect environment, Satan made a choice to lift his own name above that of The Lord (Ezekiel 28:13-19; Isaiah 14:12-15; Rev. 12:9; Luke 10:18). In that decision, he set aside the attributes of God as Sovereign Lord of Creation, and instead exalted himself. He also set

---

[58] Bruce Bradshaw, *Change across Cultures: A Narrative Approach to Social Transformation* (Grand Rapids: Baker Academic, 2002), 41.

[59] Enoch Wan, "Narrative Framework for Relational Transformational Growth" (Evangelical Missiological Society National Conference, Virtual, September 2021).

[60] Wan, "Rethinking Urban Mission in Terms of Spiritual and Social Transformational Change."

[61] "Belonging" – transformed beings in solidarity and with unity for His glory.

[62] Wan, *Diaspora Missiology*, 6-7.

aside the will/revelation of God, preferring instead to demand his own will be accomplished.

Growing from that mis-directed worship, he has become the accuser of God's people, a liar and a murderer, and the author of death (John 8:44; Heb. 2:14). At times he is subtle and understated; and at other times a roaring lion but forever his nature is to (mis-)direct the worship of Triune God with the worship of himself. His pride even went so far as to tempt the Incarnate Son of God, Jesus Christ, to worship the creature instead of the Creator.

Satan now rules a kingdom of darkness (Col. 1:13-14), and since Adam and Eve's fall, all humanity begins life in subjection to the ruler of this world (2 Cor. 4:4).

The Cross of Calvary and the Resurrection of The Son of God have made the false nature of this pretender to be visible to the rulers and principalities in heavenly places. The Cross of Calvary and the Resurrection of the Son of God also open the door for redemption (i.e., slave being bought from the marketplace for a price) for all who believe (Eph. 1:7-8; Heb. 9:15). Interculturally, Satan produces guilt, shame, and fear in those under his dominion. Redemption brings forgiveness, acceptance, and the Holy Spirit's power and protection.

Transformative leadership of Jesus Christ

A different story of change points to transformation toward godly results, the opposite of the transgressional change in the heart of Satan.

Jesus Christ, created innocent and yet not living in a perfect environment, decided as a young boy to seek the things of His Father (Luke 2:41-51). He submitted to being tempted by the evil one and was tempted in all ways that we are yet without sin (Heb. 4:13-15). He consistently refuted those temptations based on the Word of God. Philippians tells us that He submitted to the will of the Father, even to the death on the cross (Phil. 2).

Point after point, Jesus Christ chose the Father's attributes and revealed will. That approach to following the Word of God and the relationship with the Father became Jesus' form of leading His followers. His leadership brings transformation in two different but related ways:

1. That He is the Author and Finisher of our Faith (Heb. 12:2), an example who shows us how to direct our lives toward the character and attributes and revelation of the Triune God.
2. That those who believe and follow Him are given a transformed sense of direction and values in their lives: born again (John 3) and "transformed" (Romans 12) toward an imperfect and yet real life-

orientation toward the Father, Son, Spirit and their attributes and directions.

Case study of the Transformative Leadership of the Apostle Paul

From Jesus (of the Triune God) and Satan (angelic being), we now turn to apostle Paul who is a human being like us. The experience and ministry of God-honoring impactful changes: Saul of Tarsus was a religious leader who was intent on transgression prior to his drastic conversation, encountering the resurrected Lord.

This seems to be self-contradictory because he was a religious leader with intention to be ethically upright, morally correct and whole-heartedly obedient to his Jewish religion. Yet being ethical, moral, and faithful to one's religious tradition is not the same as being set on God's purposes, revelation, and character. Like Satan who exalted himself, Saul was engaged with his own definitions of righteousness and religiosity; instead of the character of Triune God and the truth as revealed by God.

There came a moment where God's grace and glory were on display with such intensity that Saul was blinded, starved, and weakened physically. Being blind for three days, he was socially isolated and helpless (Act 9). To teach him of the depth of his previous spiritual blindness, the Lord confronted Saul on the road to Damascus and this encounter led to a transformative change in holistic way: physically, volitionally and spiritually.

It was a change in the deepest levels of Paul – even to the point that his name changed from Saul to Paul. His profession changed from religious leader to an outcast among pious Jewish leaders. From his own testimony, Paul's hopes and dreams were changed, wanting only to be found in Christ. His lifestyle and life-direction changed.

The danger is to see those changes as the cause, but in fact they are the result. The cause of these changes was the transformative presence of the resurrected Christ as a relational reality in Paul's life. To know Christ and to be found in Him was the deep transformative change from Paul's side; the lifestyle changes were secondary. Jesus' presence, as noted above, brought transformation to Paul as an example of true godliness and as the power of resurrection that brings a new birth and a new creation.

Paul is a case study that shows us the human dilemma: we are born with a fallen nature that needs to be transformed by imputed righteousness of Christ. The role of faith enters because there is no human effort that can transform the fallen human heart. We need a transformation from outside: an example of life in the fullness of the Spirit and the power and new birth that come in the Spirit. Without such a transformative relationship, humanity at times ignores God and instead seeks a life of self-directed pleasure; at other times humanity may seek a righteousness that grows from human wisdom and self-effort. Neither of those is effective at bringing transformation. Interculturally, the Gospel moves us from:

- Guilty to forgiven and Holy-Spirit empowered to live righteously
- Isolated and shamed to accepted in the Beloved
- Being under bondage to the evil one to being free in Christ.

Paul illustrates that all of these shifts are interculturally relevant. The figures below are a narrative case study of the apostle Paul in terms of transformational leadership, first in terms of formation or being, then in terms of performance or doing.

#	Aspects	Relationally transformational leadership
#1 – Being: leadership formation	Dynamic interaction	Triune God as both an example and illustration of godly transformative leadership AND the power of Triune God as the cause of transformation. Father, Son, Spirit and believer in communion with the congregation of believers working together toward godly goals.
	Process	Grow in the grace and knowledge of the Lord Jesus Christ (2 Peter 3:18) – through the power of the Word, the action of the Spirit and the influence of the Body of Christ (congregations),
	Outcome	Individually growing in wisdom, grace, and spiritual maturity. Congregationally growing in Shalom and in godly influence of being salt and light to the world outside.
	Remark	Godly leadership is recognized more than developed. It is not a simple matter of taking the right classes, reading the right books, or espousing the right leadership philosophy. On the contrary, it is a matter of leading from a position of submissive relationship with Triune God, using gifts that God gives and pursuing outcomes that reflect God's character and attributes.

Figure 4-1. Relationally Transformational Leadership: Formation (Being)

#	Aspects	Relationally transformational leadership
#2 – Doing: leadership operation	Dynamic interaction	Influence more than power. God who is rightful Sovereign still often gives to creation a freedom of choice. Human leadership is also through relational influence more than through power.
	Process	**Vertical**: human leadership in connection with God's character, His Word, and His daily "manna" of presence, direction and provision. **Horizontal**: communicating the direction that Triune God makes clear to the leader in a way that facilitates the ability of followers to respond to God's attributes and will. This includes knowing the nature of the audience (cultural traits, ages, religious/political/socioeconomic situation); however, as important as that audience knowledge is, the core process is communicating and deciding with focus on God's character, attributes and will/revelation.
	Performance	Vertical: a group of people who are growing in knowledge and in daily relational interaction with Triune God. Horizontal: a group of people who demonstrate within their own relationships the peaceable fruits of righteousness, the fruit of the Spirit, and the Shalom that comes from a relationship with Triune God.
	Remark	Leadership is measured by the <u>faithfulness</u> of the leader as he/she follows God in His character, attributes and revelation/will. The desired outcome of faithfulness is <u>fruitfulness:</u> individually and corporately interacting relationally with God and with one another according to His character and attributes.

Figure 4-2. Relationally Transformational Leadership: Performance (Doing)

Popular Leadership and Relational Leadership

Listed below are definitions of leadership proposed by various authors:

- Walter C. Wright: "a relationship in which one person seeks to influence the thoughts, behaviors, beliefs, or values of another person."[63]

---

[63] Walter C. Jr. Wright, *Relational Leadership: A Biblical Model for Influence and Service*, Second edition (Downers Grove, IL: IVP Books, 2009), 8.

- Greg Ogden and Daniel Meyer: "The art of multiplying influence"[64]
- Warren Bennis: "The capacity to translate vision into reality"[65]
- John Maxwell: "Leadership is influence – nothing more, nothing less."[66]
- Margaret D. Pusch: "Seen as an activity, the process of mobilizing a group of people to accomplish a goal or fulfill a vision."[67]
- Eugene Peterson: Christian leadership is "a way of living that suffuses everything we do and are. Leadership is a way of being in the family and marriage, a way of being among friends, a way of going to work, a way of climbing mountains; most basically a way of following Jesus."[68]
- Sherwood G. Lingenfelter: Christian cross-cultural leadership is "inspiring people who come from two or more cultural traditions to participate with you (the leader or leadership team) in building a community of trust and then to follow you and be empowered by you to achieve a compelling vision of faith."[69]

Popular Leadership and Relational Transformational Leadership

Empowered by the Triune God and engendered by the leader's vision, a core organizational competency can foster competitive advantage for organizations.[70] The characteristic of visionary leadership is the style that is infectious and influential on followers who can corporately translate the leader's vision into a promising organization's future.[71]

The infectious influence of visioning by an inspirational leader on subordinates can lead to desirable organizational change, as proposed by Indian educator

---

[64] Greg Ogden and Daniel Meyer. *Leadership Essentials: Shaping Vision, Multiplying Influence, Defining Character*. (InterVarsity Press, 2009), 21.

[65] John C. Maxwell. *The 17 Essential Qualities of a Team Player: Becoming the Kind of Person Every Team Wants*. (HarperCollins Leadership, 2006), 93.

[66] John C. Maxwell, *The 21 Irrefutable Laws of Leadership Workbook: Revised and Updated*. (HarperCollins Leadership, 2007), 13.

[67] Margaret. D. Pusch, "The Interculturally Competent Global Leader,' in *The SAGE Handbook of Intercultural Competence*. Ed. Deardorff, Darla K. (SAGE, 2009), 72.

[68] Eugene Peterson, "Follow the Leader," *Fuller Focus*, Fall 2001, 31.

[69] Sherwood G. Lingenfelter, *Leading Cross-Culturally: Covenant Relationships for Effective Christian Leadership*. (Baker Academic, 2008), 21.

[70] Stephen J. Zaccaro and Deanna Banks, "Leader visioning and adaptability: Bridging the gap between research and practice on developing the ability to manage change," Wiley Online Library, 17 November 2004 https://doi.org/10.1002/hrm.20030 (Accessed Aug. 25, 2018)

[71] Burt Nanus, "Visionary Leadership: Creating a Compelling Sense of Direction for Your Organization," ERIC, 1992.

Sangeeta Sahu.[72] Theories of transformational leadership[73] and charismatic leadership[74] provide important insights on effective leadership; but most of the

---

[72] Sangeeta Sahu, Avinash Pathardikar, Anupam Kumar, (2018) "Transformational leadership and turnover: Mediating effects of employee engagement, employer branding, and psychological attachment", Leadership & Organization Development Journal, Vol. 39 Issue: 1, 82-99, Emerald Publishing Limited 2018. https://doi.org/10.1108/LODJ-12-2014-0243. (Accessed Aug. 25, 2018). The implications of the study are of utmost importance for Indian IT industries facing high voluntary turnover in recent times. Transformational leaders in teams contribute to develop employee engagement, employer branding, and psychological attachment. Imparting transformational leadership training to team leaders can help in generating psychological attachment with the employees which would go a long way.

[73] Listed below are selective references on "transformational leadership" –

- Barling, J., Weber, T. and Kelloway, E. K. 1996. "Effects of transformational leadership training on attitudinal and financial outcomes: A field experiment." *Journal of Applied Psychology*, 81: 827–832.
- Bass, B. M. "A new paradigm of leadership: An inquiry into transformational leadership," Alexandria, VA: US Army Research Institute for the Behavioral and Social Sciences. 1996.
- Lowe, K. B., Kroeck, K. G. and Sivasubramaniam, N. 1996. "Effectiveness correlates of transformational and transactional leadership: A meta-analytic review of the MLQ literature." *Leadership Quarterly*, 7: 385–425.
- Roberts, N. C. 1985. Transforming Leadership: A process of collective action. *Human Relations*, 38: 1023–1046.
- Shelley D. Dionne, Francis J. Yammarino, Leanne E. Atwater, William D. Spangler, "Transformational leadership and team performance", *Journal of Organizational Change Management*, Vol. 17 Issue: 2, 177-193, (2004) https://doi.org/10.1108/09534810410530601 (Accessed Aug. 25, 2018).
- Kendra Cherry, "Transformational Leadership: A Closer Look at the Effects of Transformational Leadership," https://www.verywellmind.com/what-is-transformational-leadership-2795313 (accessed Feb. 2, 2021).
  - Derek Farnsworth, Jennifer L. Clark, John Hall, Shannon Johnson, Allen Wysocki, and Karl Kepner, "Transformational Leadership: The Transformation of Managers and Associates." https://edis.ifas.ufl.edu/hr020 (accessed Feb. 2, 2021). They proposed four factors to transformational leadership, (also known as the "four I's"): idealized influence, inspirational motivation, intellectual stimulation, and individual consideration.

[74] Listed below are selective references on "charismatic leadership" –

- B Shamir, RJ House, MB Arthur, "The motivational effects of charismatic leadership: A self-concept based theory" - Organization science, 1993. https://pubsonline.informs.org/doi/abs/10.1287/orsc.4.4.577 (Accessed Aug. 25, 2018)
- JA Conger, RN Kanungo, "Charismatic leadership: The elusive factor in organizational effectiveness." Sage Publications, Inc. 1998 http://psycnet.apa.org/record/1988-98415-000 (Accessed Aug. 25, 2018).
- R.J. House, JM Howell, "Personality and charismatic leadership." *The Leadership Quarterly*, 1992. https://www.sciencedirect.com/science/article/pii/104898439290028E (Accessed Aug. 25, 2018).

theories are weak in the conceptualization and measurement of leadership processes.[75]

Popular paradigms of Christian ministry (i.e., programmatic, managerial and entrepreneur) in contemporary context in the west are secularized and post-Christian. Evangelical Christians are not to conform to the worldly way; instead, are to be transformed (Rom 12:1-4). Popular Christian paradigms are to be re-examined from a scriptural and theological perspectives (see extensive critique elsewhere by Enoch Wan).[76] A simple comparison of two Christian approaches is shown diagrammatically in the table below:

- SA Kirkpatrick, E. A. Locke "Direct and indirect effects of three core charismatic leadership components on performance and attitudes." *Journal of Applied Psychology*, 1996.
- D. N. Den Hartog, R.J. House, PJ Hanges. "Culture specific and cross-culturally generalizable implicit leadership theories: Are attributes of charismatic/transformational leadership universally endorsed?" *Leadership Quarterly,* 10:2, 1999)

[75] For critique of both transformational leadership and charismatic leadership, see Gary Yukl, "An Evaluative Essay on Current Conceptions of Effective Leadership," Pages 33-48 | Published online: 10 Sep 2010 https://www.sciencedirect.com/science/article/pii/S1048984399000132#! (Accessed Aug. 25, 2018)

[76] For a critique of popular paradigms (chapter 7) and a proposal of "relational paradigm" (chapters 13-14), see Enoch Wan, *Diaspora Missiology: Theory, Methodology, and Practice.* (2nd edition) IDS, 2015.

Element	Popular	Relationally Transformative
What to be achieved? (dimension)	Skills, knowledge, etc. (horizontal dimensions)	Christian transformative change (first vertical then horizontal)
Focus	Program and process	People and relationship (Christianity – true to Scripture)
Strategy	Traditional	Interactive and personal (Beings of Triune God & beings)
Success /evaluation	Measurable outcome	Not lineal/individualistic; but holistic &communal
What to be achieved	A proficient leader with followers; leaving a legacy.	An exemplary follower of Christ who inspires others (1st character + 2nd career)
Focus	Making a leader according to prevailing cultural norms; success, authority and fame	Cultivating a leader according to the Kingdom of God: God's attributes & Kingdom values. Authority is based on humility (character) and mutuality (relationship).
Strategy (dimension)	Leadership style: programmatic, managerial and entrepreneur	- Primarily vertical and secondarily horizontal relationships - Convergence of vertical and horizontal dynamism, leading to transformational changes: levels (personal & institutional) & multiple dimensions (1st vert. + 2nd horizon.) - Process: inspiration $\rightarrow$ initiative $\rightarrow$ implementation $\rightarrow$ influence (chain of transformative change)
Success/evaluation	popularity contest & quantifiable outcomes	1st Faithfulness to God vertically and 2nd fruitfulness by God's empowerment and provision horizontally

Figure 4-3. Two Christian Paradigms: Popular and Relationally Transformative[77]

---

[77] Enoch Wan. "Relational Transformational Leadership: An Asian Christian Perspective." The East-West Center for Missions Research & Development, *Asian Missions Advance*, #71 April 2021:6.

Below is a list of reflections on popular Christian leadership[78] which are often formulated based on:

- functional efficiency (even "servant" leadership)
- within a competitive context (leading companies, military, etc.) so is to "get out ahead"
- organizational skill (managerial)
- self-actualization (i.e., "be all you can be")
- evaluation that is performance-based (e.g., bonuses, leadership awards)

Relationship (especially the vertical dimension) is foundational to leadership; though it is missing or neglected from the popular Christian approach. In Christian relational and transformative approach: leaders who can translate vision (vertically received) into transformative changes on others horizontally cannot afford to exploit relationship as a means to the end (i.e., quantifiable outcomes of "success") in the leadership process.

"From a biblical perspective, **relationships are fundamental** and part of what it means to lead is to have meaningful relationships and to love those that we lead. They are not optional. This goes beyond the ethos of our relationships with others that are proscribed in Timothy and Titus, where we are told not to be overbearing, quick tempered or quarrelsome and to be gentle. Our relationships as leaders are also not simply a means to an end but are born out of a love for people and a desire to enable them also to serve and flourish."[79] (Emphasis added)

We are to heed the warning against programmatic approach and should recover the relational way as warranted in the Scriptures:

The ideas behind relational leadership are a useful reminder to us as Christians of the importance of relationship in leadership. Yet as so often is the case: a Christian worldview in leadership pre-empts many of the discoveries and developments in secular thinking; but also gives us a more balanced and rounded basis on which to lead. In the famous words of John Stott, "we need to listen to the world and to the word." In respect of leadership rather than preaching, we need to have the confidence that the Bible gives us a comprehensive and solid basis for leadership that avoids us latching onto the latest fads and fancies of the gurus and theorists.[80]

---

[78] Wan 2018:11.

[79] Jeremy Peckham, "Relational Leadership," *Evangelical Focus* (blog), April 12, 2016, http://evangelicalfocus.com/blogs/1527/Relational_Leadership.

[80] Peckham.

The figure below shows various popular approaches at two levels as compared to the relationally transformative framework at both individual and institutional level:

Level \ Approach		Programmatic/ Managerial/ Entrepreneur	Relationally Transformative Changes at Two Levels
Individual (discipleship)	Goal	Knowledge & skills	Personal relationship
	Focus	Program & procedure	Personal beings/Beings interacting
	Strategy	Event, formulaic	Relationship: 1st vertical + 2nd horizontal
	Desired outcomes	Quantitative success & measurable goal: bigger is better	Qualitative and relation-oriented growth and maturity
Institutional (pastoral & social)	Goal	Effort-optimism: • Profit, benefit, fame • Win by all means & all cost	Network & nurturing relationships: vertical + horizontal • Building up the body • Growing in Christ • God-honoring growth
	Focus	Popularity & fashionable	Triune God = foundation of being/doing & fount of blessings
	Strategy	Careful planning, systematic, strategic, striving for success	-Networking & nurturing -relationships (as track) for leadership (function: the train) to move & perform
	Desired outcomes	• Measurable outcomes of success (i.e. obsess with quantitative growth); • Increase of power, prestige & property; • Bigger is better (non-transformative change that is merely horizontal) • - Strive for success at all cost, including the sacrifice of relationship.	• All submit to the Lordship of Christ; • Guided and empowered by the Holy Spirit (who endows gifts) & Scripture • Godly relational network: edifying horizontally & God-glorifying vertically • Holistic transformative change with Kingdom-orientation

Figure 4-4. Programmatic/Managerial/Entrepreneur & Relationally Transformative Changes[81]

---

[81] Enoch Wan. "Relational Transformational Leadership: An Asian Christian Perspective." The East-West Center for Missions Research & Development, *Asian Missions Advance*, #71 April 2021:7.

The vertical and horizontal dimensions of leadership are intricately woven together; its priority is vertically Christo-centric (i.e., being, becoming and belonging); yet both vertical and horizontal are to be included:

"When we think about "Relational Leadership," viewed from God's perspective, we might consider that His concern ultimately is with the quality of both our underlined vertical and horizontal relationships, rather than just the material outcomes of what we do as an organization..." (Emphasis added)[82]

We are to be relation-oriented; rather than task-oriented: "Being more deeply relational may also require a shift of emphasis from the task-orientated nature of Western management practice to allow time and provide the context for developing relationships..."[83]

The table below is a comparison of popular approaches (i.e., programmatic/ managerial/ entrepreneur) in Christian leadership with relationally transformational leadership.

Approach Level	Aspects	Popular ministry	Relationally transformational leadership
#1 – individual discipleship	Purpose	Knowledge, skills	Enriched relationships vertical + horizontal), spiritual maturity, God-honoring growth for Kingdom-purpose
	Focus	Program	People, process & relationships
	Strategy	Systematic transmission of knowledge & skills	Relational modeling & transformative process: God → leader → followers
	Evaluation	Quantifiable outcomes & numerical success	1st quality of spirituality & Kingdom-outcomes + 2nd institutional growth
#2 – institutional/Social	Purpose	Expansion of power, prestige & property	Enriched relationship, spiritual maturity, God-honoring accomplishments
	Focus	Program, enterprise & management efficiency	People & process; both vertical & horizontal relationships
	Strategy	Successful program, well-managed system, profitable enterprise	Relational leadership with transformative process for God-honoring changes & faithful/fruitful outcomes
	Evaluation	Worldly success & fame (mere horizontally)	Christ-like character individually and God-honoring growth institutionally

---

[82] Enoch Wan. "Relational Transformational Leadership: An Asian Christian Perspective." The East-West Center for Missions Research & Development, *Asian Missions Advance*, #71 April 2021:8.
[83] Peckham, Jeremy. "*Relational Leadership.*"

Figure 4-5. Popular Approaches vs. Relationally Transformational Leadership at Two Levels[84]

Leadership and relationality are closely tied together as explained in the quotation below: ע ם7ם5ט4 יכתוב

> Regarding the application of truth to leadership, leadership skills and behaviors must be built on the foundation of who we are. As an example, Gene Getz concludes, "the most important for selecting local church leadership is spiritual qualifications."[85] Later, Getz speaks out against emphasizing numbers by saying, "the true test of a man's qualifications for church leadership must be based on 'quality' –– not 'quantity.'"[86] Simply put, the best way for leaders to lead others is to mirror God's own character being continually built in their lives (Ex. 34:6-7; Deut. 10:17-18).[87]

The diagram below shows the vertical and horizontal dimension of leadership in operation.

---

[84] Enoch Wan. "Relational Transformational Leadership: An Asian Christian Perspective." The East-West Center for Missions Research & Development, *Asian Missions Advance*, #71 April 2021:8.

[85] Gene A. Getz, *Sharpening the Focus of the Church* (Chicago: Moody Press, 1974), 118.

[86] Getz, *Sharpening the Focus of the Church*, 119.

[87] Enoch Wan and Jace Cloud, *Doxological Missiology: Theory, Motivation, and Practice.* Western Academic Publishers. 2022, 93.

Vertical	Vertical + Horizontal	Horizontal
Leadership is a gift from God (Romans 12:1-16)	Leadership is for servants (Mark 10:35-45)	Leadership is serving rather than ruling (1 Kings 11-12)
Leadership finds success in seeking God, not power (2 Chron. 26:1-23)	Leadership serves at the pleasure of God (1 Samuel 10: 17-27)	Leadership is responsible for the growth of people (Ezekiel 34:1-10)
Leadership celebrates the coming King (2 Samuel 6:1-23)	Leadership seeks continual renewal (Col. 1:9-14)	Leadership is for the empowerment of others (Ephesians 4:1-13)
Leadership trusts God when risking decisions (Acts 15:1-29)	Leadership leaves a legacy (2 Sam. 23:1-7)	Leadership manages partnerships (1 Kings 5:1-12)
Leadership reflects the character of God (Galatians 5:13-26)	N/A	Leadership requires courageous followers (2 Samuel 19:1-8)
Leadership envisions God's future (Revelation 20-22)	N/A	Leadership contributes to Christian community (Philippians 2:1-11)
N/A	N/A	Leadership is responsible for the use of resources (Genesis 41:15-57)
N/A	N/A	Leadership is responsible for the use of time (Luke 10:38-42)
N/A	N/A	Leadership models integrity of character (1 Corinthians 13:1-13)

Figure 4-6. Dimensions of Leadership in Operation[88]

The figure below lists out the interaction between personal Beings (the Trinity) and beings (Christians within the Church), leading to transformational change at personal and collective levels.

---

[88] Adapted from "The Theology of Leadership" in Walter C. Wright. *Relational Leadership: A Biblical Model for Influence and Service.* InterVarsity Press, 2009:11.

Connection / Person	Relationship	Example Scriptures
Father	Individual: Fatherhood	Matthew 6:9; Our Father in heaven
Father	Corporate: Fatherhood	1 Peter 2:17; Love the brotherhood
Son	Individual: Lordship	Colossians 2:6; as you received Christ Jesus the Lord, so walk in him,
Son	Corporate: Headship	Ephesians 4:14-15; grow up into Christ, the head
Holy Spirit	Individual: body as temple	1 Corinthians 6:19-20; your body is a temple of the Holy Spirit within you
Holy Spirit	Corporate: church as temple	1 Corinthians 3:16-17; you (plural) are God's temple; Spirit dwells in you (plural)
Church	Family	1 Timothy 5:1-2; Older man as father, younger as brother, etc.
Church	Koinonia	1 Corinthians 12:24-27; Body of Christ, individually members
Church	Ecclesia	1 Timothy 3:15; Household of God is church of the Living God

Figure 4-7. Narrative Framework and Transformational Change

The figure below shows relational transformational leadership for change in two dimensions: vertical and horizontal.

Change Dimensions	TRANSFORMATIONAL CHANGE
Vertical + horizontal	**Transcendental & transformational –** Divine + personal (will) *Perichoresis* transformed (being + doing)
Horizontal	**High level:** interaction – formed (being) **Mid-level:** psychological, behavioral and social – forming & reformed (doing) **Lower level:** knowledge - informed (knowing)

Figure 4-8. Relational Transformational Leadership for Change in two Dimensions.[89]

Relational Intercultural Leadership

As shown in Figure 2-7, and repeated below, leader and follower(s) come with different cultural backgrounds, yet both have been transformed to have a new life and can enjoy the indwelling of the Holy Spirit. Yet providentially they meet interculturally with different roles and responsibilities as "leader" and "follower(s)." From left to right, "being" is the beginning of the process of transformational change, from "belonging" moving towards "becoming."

---

[89] Enoch Wan, "Relational Transformational Leadership — An Asian Christian Perspective," *Asian Missions Advance* (2021), http://www.asiamissions.net/asian-missions-advances/6.

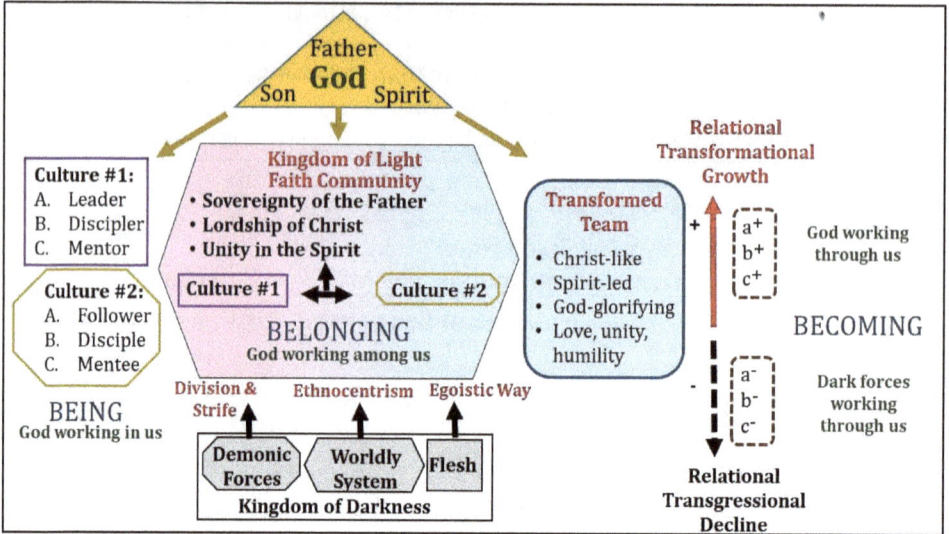

Figure 4-9. The Practice and Process of Relational Intercultural Leadership

As shown in the figure above, there are three phases of transformational change: being → belonging and becoming in intercultural leadership.

Since the focus of this chapter is on "intercultural leadership," therefore leader and follower(s) are realistically coming from different cultural backgrounds and/or ethnic origins. However, both leader and follower(s) are people transformed by the power of the Gospel unto salvation (Rom 1: 16) by the Triune God; regardless of their ethnic background of being Jew or gentile. However, they are different ontologically in their "being" due to the variation of degree and intensity of "God working in us." Leaders are more mature in spirituality, more Christ-like in character, and empowered with the gift of leadership.

The figure above realistically shows that forces from the kingdom of darkness can derail the process of transformational growth and push instead toward transgressional change. Outworking of that transgressional change includes: (a) division and strife from demonic forces spiritually; (b) ethnocentrism from worldly system externally; (c) egoistic way from the flesh/carnal nature internally.

Summary

In this introductory chapter for section 3, we provide a narrative study of the transgressional leadership of Satan, transformative leadership of Jesus

Christ and the apostle Paul. The figures below are helpful to recap the major elements covered in this chapter.

Element	Relationally Transgressive	Relationally Transformative
What to be achieved? (dimension)	A form of godliness that denies the power of the Cross; seeks self-directed righteousness and/or self-serving pleasure	Christian transformative change (first vertical then horizontal)
Focus	Licentiousness or a Law-based series of rules	People and relationship (Christianity – true to Scripture)
Strategy	Self-focused and self-pleasing	Interactive and personal (Beings of Triune God & beings)
Success/ evaluation	Protection of pride, riches, pleasures	Not lineal/individualistic; but holistic &communal
What to be achieved	Accumulation of riches, power, and the praise of people	An exemplary follower of Christ who inspires others (1st character + 2nd career)
Focus	Cultivating a leader according to the World's values or developing a form of godliness that denies very power of the cross.	Cultivating a leader according to the Kingdom of God: God's attributes & Kingdom values. Authority is based on humility (character) and mutuality (relationship).
Strategy (dimension)	Deception and Distraction - (Satan as a liar from the beginning) Force (Satan as a murderer from the beginning)	- Primarily vertical and secondarily horizontal relationships - Convergence of vertical and horizontal dynamism, leading to transformational changes: levels (personal & institutional) & multiple dimensions (1st vertical + 2nd horizontal) Process: inspiration → initiative → implementation → influence (chain of transformative change)
Success/ evaluation	Seeking contentment, human happiness but missing God's Shalom	1st Faithfulness to God vertically and 2nd fruitfulness by God's empowerment and provision horizontally

Figure 4-10. Two Types of Change: Relationally Transgressive and Transformative

The figure below shows relationally transgressive and transformative changes at both individual and institutional level:

Level ╲ Approach		Relationally transgressive changes	Relationally transformative changes at 2 levels
Individual (followership)	Goal	Exaltation of self and of evil beings (Luke 4:1-12)	Personal relationship
	Focus	Power, riches, comfort	Personal brings/Beings interacting
	Strategy	Position, hierarchy, gathering of possessions	Relationship: 1st vertical + 2nd horizontal
	Desired outcomes	Matthew 6:32 – what the nations seek	Qualitative and relation-oriented growth and maturity
Institutional (Leadership)	Goal	A physical life on earth that is comfortable and free of problems. An eternity (if one exists) that is also comfortable, free of problems; a paradise without earthly difficulties	Network & nurturing relationships: vertical + horizontal • Building up the body • Growing in Christ • God-honoring growth
	Focus	Self as the direct focus (riches, power) or self as the indirect focus of benefits from spiritual/ religious activity	Triune God = foundation of being/doing & fount of blessings
	Strategy	Direct people's attention to the things of this world: deception by the deceitfulness of riches, or distraction by so many preoccupations	-Networking & nurturing -relationships (as track) for leadership (function: the train) to move & perform
	Desired outcomes	Feeling good about oneself and receiving the benefits of riches, exaltation, power	• All submit to the Lordship of Christ; • Guided and empowered by the Holy Spirit (who endows gifts) & Scripture • Godly relational network: edifying horizontally & God-glorifying vertically • Holistic transformative change with Kingdom-orientation

Figure 4-11. Relationally Transgressive and Transformative Changes at Two Levels

The next three chapters will discuss the practice of intercultural leadership and the process of transformational change in terms of being (Chapter 5), belonging (Chapter 6) and becoming (Chapter 7).

CHAPTER 5
Being in Intercultural Leadership

Introduction

In this chapter, the focus is on "being" in the practice of intercultural leadership – the "point" of beginning in the "process of transformational change."

Purpose of this chapter

The purpose of this chapter is to answer the question "who are interacting" by narratively describing "being" as found on the left side of Figure 4-9, the beginning point of the three phases of transformational change: being → belonging → becoming (in the practice of intercultural leadership). In addition to the linear narrative of transformational change for growth, this chapter will provide a narrative description of the synchronic view of the first phase on "being."

"BEING" OF INTERCULTURAL LEADERSHIP: MULTI-LAYERS NARRATIVE

From a linear perspective, "being" is the starting "point" of the "process" of transformational change/growth in 3 phases. The figure below is a synchronic description of the "being" phase of the process of transformational change. As shown in the diagram below, there are 3 layers in "intercultural leadership" and "A" is at the core of "being."

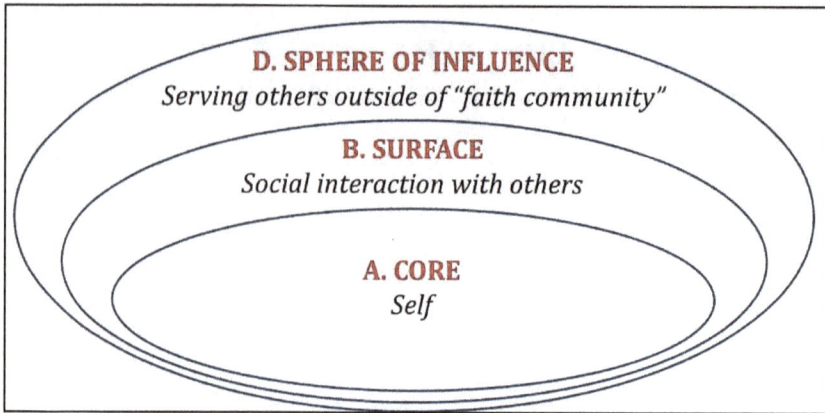

Figure 5-1. Multi-layers Narrative of Intercultural Leadership

The following quotation underscores this point, as shown in the figure above:

> 'God is initiator of transformations, even if He is not recognized as such. Transformation affects us at the level of 'being' (including worldview, character, and identity) and affects our relationships with God, ourselves and others, and how we feel, know and act within those relationships. Transformations can occur as a point and/or a process. Mezirow's 10 steps are helpful in understanding a generalized process of transformation." [90]

The figure below is an expansion of Figure 2-7 which shows the basic concept of transformational change: transformational power from the Triune God comes through the transformed leader who became an agent of transformational power (channel of blessings) impacting/influencing follower(s).

---

[90] Gimple & Wan, *Covenant transformative Learning Theory and Practice for Mission.* Western Academic Publishers. 2021:176.

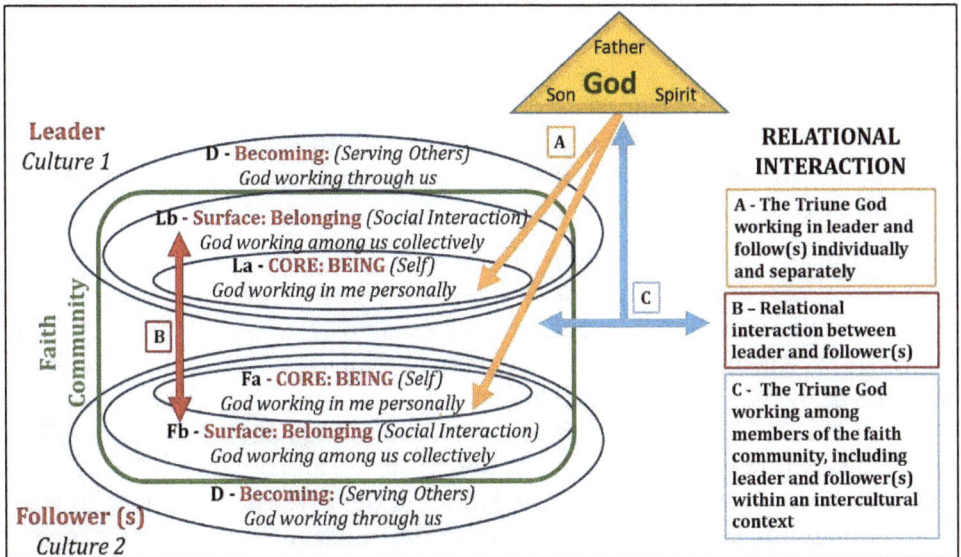

Figure 5-2. Intercultural Leadership in Action

Note the following elements and relationships described in the above figure:

- LEADER
  - La – Core: being (self) – God working in me personally
  - Lb - Surface: belong (social interaction) – God working among us collectively
  - D - Sphere of influence (serving others) – God working through us, beyond ourselves
- FOLLOWER
  - Fa – Core: being (self) – God working in me personally
  - Fb - Surface: belong (social interaction) – God working among us collectively
  - D - Sphere of influence (serving others) – God working through us, beyond ourselves
- RELATIONAL INTERACTION
  - A - The Triune God working in leader and follower(s) individually and separately
  - B – Relational interaction between leader and follower(s)
  - C - The Triune God working among members of the faith community, including leader and follower(s) within an intercultural context

"La" is at the "core" ("being") of the leader. The "self" of the leader is to be changed by the transformational power of God working in him/her personally to shape his "character." Unfortunately, the matter of "character" is not a key

61

factor in publications on popular literature on Christian leadership because it is difficult to discern and quantify/measure.

However, human behaviors are derived from their intensions, which are derived from their attitudes/values, which are ultimately derived from their beliefs (character). And so, while these are all interconnected, objective discernment of character is challenging.[91]

Since the focus of this chapter is on "intercultural leadership," therefore within such context leader and follower(s) are realistically coming from different cultural backgrounds and/or ethnic origins. However, both leader and follower(s) are people transformed by the power of the Gospel unto salvation (Rom 1: 16) by the Triune God; regardless of their ethnic background of being Jew or gentile. They both can experience "God working in us" (See Figure 5-2 arrow-A) separately prior to the encounter with one and others, but providentially interacting with one and other in the pattern of leader-follower.

They share the experience of God's salvation and transformational change (as shown by arrow "A" in Figure 5-2): from darkness to light, and from the power of Satan to God (Acts 26:10).

We bring in the vertical dimension from which the dynamism for transformation is Trinitarian: Father - "Fount of blessing" and "source of wisdom" (James 1:5-18); Son – Savior and Lord (Col 1:15-20); HS – regeneration, inspiration/illumination (Titus 3:5; 2 Tim. 3:16; John 16:13-14).[92]

Realistically leader and follower(s) cannot avoid cultural gap, ethnic diversity, and language barrier. This ontological fact can be both a challenge and opportunity when interacting, in addition to difference in role: leader and follower(s). Challenges include ethnocentrism,[93] cultural clash, linguistic barrier, etc. This phase of "being" is the "beginning point" of the long "process of transformational change" in the practice of intercultural leadership.

In the context where intercultural leadership is being practiced, they are different ontologically in their "being" due to the variation of degree and intensity of "God working in us." Leaders are expected to be more mature in spirituality, more Christ-like in character, and being empowered by the Holy

---

[91] Enoch Wan and Jace Cloud, *Doxological Missiology: Theory, Motivation, and Practice.* Western Academic Publishers. 2022:94.

[92] Enoch Wan. "Relational Transformational Leadership: An Asian Christian Perspective." The East-West Center for Missions Research & Development, *Asian Missions Advance*, #71 April 2021:2.

[93] Enoch Wan,, "Ethnocentrism" *Evangelical Dictionary of World Missions*. (Edited by Scott Moreau). Grand Rapids: Baker Books. 2000: 324-325.

Spirit with the gift of leadership (1 Cor. 12:28 and Rom 12:8). Intercultural leadership practitioners are expected to be like the apostle Paul who experienced transformative change in a holistic way: physically, volitionally, and spiritually (Act 9, 22).

Summary

In this chapter, the multi-layers of the "being" of leaders are explained and discussed briefly as the point of beginning of the process and the preparation for transformational change for growth in three phases.

CHAPTER 6
Belonging in Intercultural Leadership

Introduction

Immediately following the last chapter on "being," the focus of this chapter is on "belonging" in the practice of intercultural leadership, i.e., the "process" of transformational change.

Purpose of this Chapter

This chapter, on "belonging" in the practice of intercultural leadership, is an attempt to answer the question of interaction between personal Beings/beings: "how are they interacting and in what context?"

Intercultural Education Leading to Growth

As a process of transformational change in terms of "belonging," transformative change in the follower(s) is to take place in terms of "intercultural education" which is defined by Enoch Wan as follows:

"It is the formal/informal/non-formal process whereby the educator interacts relationally with the learner towards development/enrichment in 'being' and 'doing' (i.e., multidimensional such as cognitive, affective, volitional...etc.) within a cross-cultural context." [94]

There are four assumptions embedded in the above definition:

- **Ontologically:** Delimiting to the context of personal Beings/beings and the best way of learning is through relational interaction.
- **Epistemologically:** Subjective and objective dimensions are critically different, and yet both should be included.
- **Theoretically:** Relational perspective is preferred to other perspective (e.g., rationalistic, behavioral, communicative, and pragmatic) and the ideal development is towards positive change.

---

[94] Enoch Wan. Unpublished lecture notes from IE701: Intercultural Education, Western Seminary, Portland, OR. Spring 2019.

- **Existentially:** "Doing" is not to be separated from "being" for there is a dynamic interplay between the participants of relational interaction between the two.[95]

Ethno-relationality within Intercultural Context

On the left-hand side of Figure 4-9, leader and follower(s) are identified to be from different cultural backgrounds. Without the transformational power of the Triune God, leader and follower(s) are within the kingdom of darkness, they have division and strife from demonic forces. They conform to the world and operate with ethnocentrism and act selfishly/egoistically being ruled by the "flesh" (carnal nature). Being transformed by the power of the Triune God, leader and follower(s) have new identity (i.e., sonship in Christ, citizen of the Kingdom, children of light, etc.) and new unity (i.e., one faith and one hope, members of the body of Christ, temple of the Holy Spirit, etc.) and new humility (i.e., servant, saved sinner by grace, Christ-like character, Spirit-guided demeanor, etc.) They should replace ethnocentrism with ethno-relationality which is defined as "a reciprocal and dialogical posture in recognizing the presence of other beings of different cultures as differentiated and connected and engaging in dialogues with one another."[96] The goal of ethno-relationality is to develop more authentic, intimate, and creative relationships with God vertically and others horizontally. The figure below shows the process of shifting from "ethnocentrism" → "ethno-relationality."

---

[95] Enoch Wan. Unpublished lecture notes from IE701: Intercultural Education, Western Seminary, Portland, OR. Spring 2019.

[96] Enoch Wan & Siu Kuen Sonia Chan. "Contextualization the Asian Way." *Asian Missions Advance.* 2023:9.

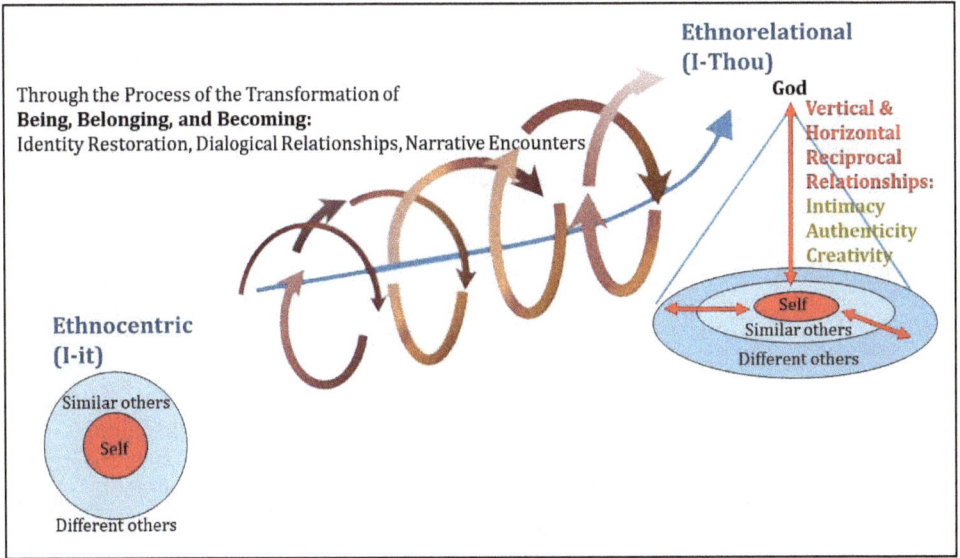

Figure 6-1. From Ethnocentrism to Ethno-relationality

Intercultural Leadership in Action

The two diagrams below show the integration of two paradigms: relational interactionism and transformational change in two stages: general leadership →intercultural leadership. The figure below shows transformational change from left to right in three states (i.e., being → belonging → becoming) and three processes (i.e., separately → together to form the Church and enjoy fellowship → consequently emerge into a new state of being in partnership, to witness and for God's glory.)

	BEING	BELONGING	BECOMING
STATE	God working **in** us Personally & separately	God working **among** us: through interactions collectively	God working **through** us: consequence of being together in new state
	- →		
PROCESS	vertically connected separately	vertical + horizontal interactions	CONSEQUENCE
	Transformed by Triune God: individuality / identity	Context: *ecclesia* (called out ones), *koinonia* (fellowship, communication	New state of 'being' συνεταιρισμός (partnership), μάρτυρας (witness), δόξα (God-glorifying),

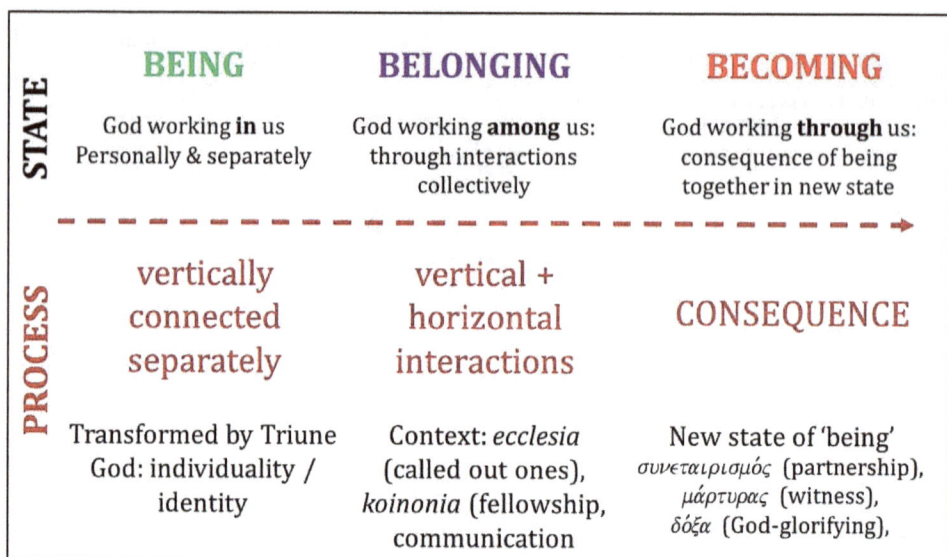

Figure 6-2. Relational Realism and Transformational Change

In the figure below, the upper part shows leader and follower(s), originally from different cultures but entering the "belonging" phase: interacting with one and other within an intercultural context, vertically submitting to the sovereignty of the Father, under the lordship of Christ and indwelt by the Holy Spirit. They become members of the faith community (the Church) and bless one and another horizontally through fellowship and God-centered communication. Despite cultural differences and possible language barriers, they interact with humility, mutuality and unity horizontally. There is a transfusion of vertical and horizontal dynamism leading to transformational change as described below:

Being different from Mezirow's focus on horizontal relationships that foster transformative learning, in this paper we want to emphasize the interactive relationship with a faith community as well. It is not simply a series of one-on-one relationships that foster transformation. Interaction with the larger group – the Church, local congregations and the faith community of Christians – is also key to transformation, especially to cyclical multiplication of leaders.[97]

---

[97]Enoch Wan. "Relational Transformational Leadership: An Asian Christian Perspective." The East-West Center for Missions Research & Development, *Asian Missions Advance*, #71 April 2021:3.

The lower part of the figure below shows "relational intercultural development in leadership" at personal and group levels. "Belonging" can be dyadic and /or collective. The following quotation underscores this point well. Christian understanding of transformational change includes the transcendent Triune God and the transformational power of the Father, Son, and Holy Spirit in the lives of individual believers and the Christian Church; not merely at the horizontal level of humanistic efforts of cognitive information, psychological formation and behavioral reform, and socio-cultural formation in enculturation, socialization and maturation. It is God at work both in and through His people that brings transformation: at times His involvement in the individual life of a leader (single believer), and at times as He works through the gathered Church. The transformative nature of Christian life bears fruit both in the individual and in the Church: the impact of transformation takes place both through His immediate agency and as He works through His Church. Therefore, transformational change can take place at two levels (individual and organizational) and two dimensions.[98]

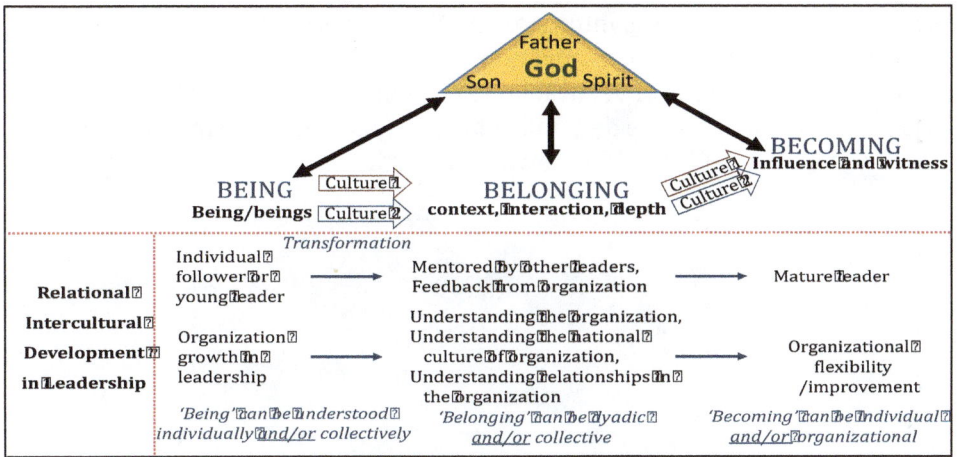

Figure 6-3. Intercultural Leadership in Action

The growth in the follower(s) according to Figure 2-5: begins with divine aid from the Trinity who is the source of transformational power being channeled through a transformed/godly leader (individually) and the faith community (collectively). However, an important factor is the positive attitude toward change and degree of receptivity for growth in the follower(s). Spiritual growth

---

[98] Enoch Wan. "Relational Transformational Leadership: An Asian Christian Perspective." The East-West Center for Missions Research & Development, *Asian Missions Advance*, #71 April 2021:6.

is not merely the result of one-on-one relationship, but largely from the Body of Christ (Rom. 12; 1 Cor. 12; Eph. 4) especially multiplication of leaders cyclically.[99]

From Figure 5-2, relational interaction:

- "A" is Triune God vertically transforming La and Fa separately in the "being" phase at the core (God working in us).
- "B" is at the surface/external/social level showing leader and follower(s) interacting with one and other collectively (God working among us) within an intercultural context with the complexity of multiple factors, i.e., cultural differences, ethnic diversity, language barrier, etc.
- "C" is the Triune God working among members of the faith community, including leader and follower(s) within an intercultural context

Summary

In this chapter "belonging" in the practice of intercultural leadership as the process of transformational change in the intercultural context where a godly/transformed leader is interacting with follower(s). It is an attempt to answer the question "how are they interacting and in what context?" It features: (a) the merging of vertical and horizontal dimensions of interactions; (b) the transfusion of divine dynamics through godly/transformed leader to impact on follower(s) for change towards growth.

---

[99] Wan & Hedinger, "Transformative Ministry for the Majority Context." *Occasional Bulletin.* 2018.

CHAPTER 7
Becoming in Intercultural Leadership

INTRODUCTION

In this chapter, the focus is on "becoming" in the practice of intercultural leadership. In terms of interacting personal Beings/beings, this chapter is an attempt to answer the question: "what influence do they have on each other and beyond?"

Purpose of this chapter

The purpose of this chapter is to provide a narrative of "becoming" in the practice of intercultural leadership, leading to transformational change for growth. It is an attempt to answer the question on the interactive pattern of personal Beings/beings in the context of intercultural leadership: what influence do they have on each other and beyond, leading to transformational growth?

The Process/Layers and Outcome of Transformational Growth

In this last chapter of Section 3 of the book, it is fitting to use the figure below to summarize the paradigm of transformational growth in general. The linear progression towards transformational growth is a **diachronic process** (left side-red):

being (God working in us)
→ belonging (God working among us)
→ becoming (God working through us and beyond us)

The progression towards transformational growth has multi-layers (a **synchronic development** (left side – in **purple**):

"self" at the core (internal individuality)
→ social (interacting externally)
→ sphere of influence: serving others outside of the faith community in Christ's name, by His power, for His sake, and to His glory[100]

---

[100] See Enoch Wan. *Diaspora Missions to International Students.* Western Seminary Press. 2019: chapter 2.

The listing above includes two perspectives of transformational change leading to growth:

- the process (linear and diachronic)
- multi-layers (analytical and synchronic)

The figure below is a visual explanation of these two perspectives of transformational change toward growth.

Process & Layers ➡	Outcome of Transformational Growth		
interactive process of transfusion: divine + human (vertical + horizontal)	transformative relationships: • with God vertically • leader & follower(s) horizontally		
ethnocentric/egoistic ➡	ethno-relational, godliness, Christ-like character, Spirit-led lifestyle, God-glorifying witness		
Being (...in us) (self: inner core)	• individuality • cultural identity	• authenticity	• new identity
Belonging (...among us) (social: external)	• ethno-relational interaction • perichoresis experience	• love & humility • intimacy & mutuality	• new relationships
Becoming (...through us & beyond us) (sphere of influence: serving others)	• divine encounters • not worldly conformation but divine transformation	• reciprocity • unity & shalom (peace & harmony)	• personal/ spiritual transformation • social transformation

Figure 7-1. The Process and Outcome of Transformational Growth in Intercultural Leadership

The Process/Layers of "becoming" –
Transformational Growth in Intercultural Leadership

We will now deal with the linear/processual aspect of transformational change, followed by a discussion of the multi-layers aspect of transformational change:

The process of transformational growth in intercultural leadership

The process of transformational change toward growth is of God's desire and by His design as stated in the verses below:

And we know that in all things God works for the good of those who love him, who have been called according to his purpose. For those God foreknew he also predestined to be conformed to the image of his Son, that he might be the firstborn among many brothers and sisters. (Rom. 8:28-29).

At the beginning **phase ("being")** of the transformational process, both leader and follower(s) have their own individuality and cultural identity. God is working in them both individually and personally to bring in transformational change by reconciliation and regeneration (i.e., relational interaction "A" in Figure 5-2. As shown in Figure 7-1, individuality, and cultural identity of participants [leader and follower] move towards authenticity).

Providentially, the leader (La) of Figure 5-2 and follower(s) (Fa) encounter one and another in the relational pattern "B" - leadership and followership. They then enter the **"belonging" phase** interacting with one and other relationally (i.e., relational interaction "B" in Figure 5-2) and being part of the faith community (rectangle in green). If both leader and follower(s) practice the virtue of love and humility, with intimacy & mutuality (Figure 7-1), then it will lead to new relationships of "belonging" (i.e., children of God, members of the body of Christ, part of the temple of the Holy Spirit, members of the chosen nation, loyal priesthood, etc.)[101] At this point, we see the process of transfusion of divine and human dynamics: the transformative power of the Triune God coming through the transforming agents of godly leader (dyadic) and nurturing faith community (collective and multi-dimensional), positively impacting follower(s) towards transformative change. They can also enjoy the perichoresis experience (Figure 7-1) as described below in 1 John 4:11-12: "No one has ever seen God; but if we love one another, God lives in us and his love is made

---

[101] See detailed discussion in two publications on new relationships of God's people in terms of "belonging" as the focus of this chapter:
- Charles van Engen. *God's Missionary People: Rethinking the Purpose of the Local Church.* Grand Rapids: Baker. 1991.
- David E. Stevens. *God's New Humanity: A Biblical Theology of Multiethnicity for the Church.* Oregon: Wipf & Stock. 2012.

complete in us." They can be transformed from the emphasis of individuality to relational intimacy, from self-centered orientation to mutuality.

According to Figure 7-1, the **"becoming"** phase can be narratively described as "God working through us and beyond us." The transforming power of the Triune God can change both leader and follower(s) from ethnocentric/egoistic to become ethno-relational and godly. Instead of conformation to the worldly way, the divine transformational power channeled through godly leaders can change the follower(s) to become Christ-like in character, Spirit-led in lifestyle and God-glorifying witness as stated by Jesus Christ: "A new command I give you: Love one another. As I have loved you, so you must love one another. By this everyone will know that you are my disciples." (John 13:34-35) "Becoming" in the process of transformational change for growth will have the outcome of Christian reciprocity, Spirit-endowed unity and divinely granted *shalom*[102] which is a key element in "social transformation" being defined in Chapter 5 and quoted below:

> **Social Transformation** (being → belonging[103] → becoming): God working through an aggregate of transformed Christians (at both individual and institutional levels) spiritually (saving souls) and socially (ushering in **_shalom_**) for redemption, reconciliation, and transformation[104] in a process of three phases: being, belonging, and becoming.

For a detailed discussion on "spiritual transformation" and "social transformation," see Enoch Wan. "Rethinking Urban Mission in Terms of Spiritual and Social Transformational Change." MSG/WAMS Biennial International Conference - October 27-29, 2021.

The multi-layers transformational growth in intercultural leadership

At the **core of "being"** is the internal "self" of both leader and follower(s) as shown in Figure 6-1. Each experiences God's "working in us" personally (i.e., relational interaction – "A" in regeneration) with the new "self" or Paul's expression of "inner man" (2 Cor. 4:16; Eph. 3:16; Rom 7:22–23).

The dynamism of change is that it originates vertically from the Triune God and is ushered in horizontally on leaders and follower(s) alike (i.e., relational

---

[102] See the discussion on *shalom* by Bryant L. Myers. *Walking with the Poor: Principles and Practices of Transformational Development*, Maryknoll, NY: Orbis Books, 2011:80-84. Myers emphasized relational transformation from the Triune God, extended to community and neighbors. Myers viewed that *Shalom* and wholeness are closely tied together in *Health, Healing and Shalom*, B .L. Myers, E. Dufault-Hunter, & I. B. Voss. (eds.) Pasadena: William Carey Library, 2015.

[103] "Belonging" – transformed beings in solidarity and with unity for His glory.

[104] Wan, *Diaspora Missiology*, 6-7.

interaction "A" in Figure 5-2). Transformation of "being" is thus the ushering in of a new identity: from I-it → I-Thou.[105]

Externally at **the "surface" level**, there is relational interaction ("B" in Figure 5-2) between leader and follower(s) of two different roles. For detailed discussion of leadership in Asian context, see Enoch Wan: "Relational Transformational Leadership: An Asian Christian Perspective."[106] Both leader and follower(s) are members of the faith community (rectangle in green of Figure 5-2). God's transformational power came through the agent of leader to impact follower(s) for positive change. In addition, the gift of leadership (Rom. 12 and 1 Cor. 12) from God enables leader ("Lb" of Figure 5-2) to impact follower(s) (Fb) for positive change towards growth. In addition, the faith community (rectangle in green – Figure 5-2) provides nurture and sustaining support for the follower(s) changing towards growth. At this level, "perichoresis" carries the spiritual interaction within the Trinity into the vertical relationship between God and man characterized in "shared interiority."

According to John Jefferson Davis, "perichoresis can be understood to involve a relationship of shared interiority, in which two (or more) persons share, at a deep level, their inner lives with one another. It involves an 'opening of the heart' to the other, a giving of permission to the other to 'get inside' my life."[107] In addition, Gimple and Wan propose "Perichoretic discourse as part of the process of restoring shalom."[108]

With the divine aid of Triune God, (relational interaction – "C" of Figure 5-2), the sphere of influence of a godly leader enables them to serve others, within and beyond the faith community (see Figure 7-1). According to Figure 4-10, godly leader and follower(s) are transformed into a team of powerful witnesses through their Christ-like character, Spirit-led lifestyle, self-less love, Spirit-granted unity in multi-layers.[109] In addition, they are:

- an imperfect reflection of the Perfection of the Triune God in unity/harmony → multi-level relational transformation

---

[105] Enoch Wan & Siu Kuen Sonia Chan. "Contextualization the Asian Way." *Asian Missions Advance.* 2023:10.

[106] Enoch Wan, "Relational Transformation Leadership - An Asian Christian Perspective," *Asian Missions Advance*, April 2021, http://www.asiamissions.net/relational-transformational-leadership-an-asian-christian-perspective/.

[107] John Jefferson Davis, "What Is 'Perichoresis' – and Why Does It Matter? Perichoresis as Properly Basic to the Christian Faith," Evangelical Review of Theology 39, no. 2 (April 2015): 146.

[108] Ryan Gimple & Enoch Wan. *Covenant Transformative Learning: Theory and Practice for Mission.* Western Academic Publishers. 2021:260.

[109] Enoch Wan, "Relational Transformational Leadership: An Asian Christian Perspective." Asian Missions Advance, April 2021: 2.

- horizontally and internally interacting in love and with harmony[110]

The **sphere of influence** of godly leader who can mobilize follower(s) to serve others beyond the faith community[111] in terms of spiritual and social transformation. [112] "Becoming" is spiritual transformation[113] as defined in Chapter 5 and quoted below:

Spiritual Transformation (being → belonging → becoming) - God working in us, working among us and working through us for the fulfillment of His will to grow and glorify Him.

The sphere of influence of godly leader includes the ushering in shalom[114] which is closely tied with "mission," according to Enoch Wan's definition:

"Christians (individuals) and the Church (institutional) continuing on and carrying out the *mission Dei* of the Triune God ('mission') at both individual and institutional levels spiritually (saving soul) and socially (ushering in shalom[115]) for redemption, reconciliation, and transformation ('missions')."[116]

Along with transformed follower(s), godly leader's sphere of influence can be extended beyond the faith community by powerful God-glorifying witness:

Leaders need to know the desired result of their organization in order to accurately measure success or failure. One must ask: what is the purpose of our organization? Ephesians 4:12 defines the desired outcome of church

---

[110] Enoch Wan. "Relational Transformational Leadership: An Asian Christian Perspective," 3.

[111] A helpful reference on this is: Ruth Haley Barton, *Life Together in Christ: Experiencing Transformation in Community* (Downers Grove: InterVarsity Press, 2014.

[112] "Spiritual transformation" and "social transformation" are the major focus of the paper by Enoch Wan. "Rethinking Urban Mission in Terms of Spiritual and Social Transformational Change." MSG/WAMS Biennial International Conference - October 27-29, 2021.

[113] Ruth Haley Barton's understanding of "spiritual transformation as "the process by which Christ is formed in us -- for the glory of God, for the abundance of our own lives and for the sake of others."

[114] According to Nicholas Wolterstorff, shalom can be narratively described as "the human being dwelling in peace with all of his or her relationship with God, with self, with fellow, with nature are peaceful." See Nicholas Wolterstorff, *Until Justice and Peace Embrace*. Eerdmans, 1983:71.

[115] Wan notes that "shalom" is the context of total wellness in which created humanity can reach his/her full potential and properly respond to God and his message relationally (Jer. 29:7; 1 Tim. 2:1–5).

[116] Wan, Enoch. "Diaspora Missiology and International Student Ministry (ISM)." Diaspora Missions to International Students. Ed., Enoch Wan. Portland, OR: Western Seminary Press, 2019. Chapter 2.

ministry: "for the equipping of the saints for the work of service, to the building up of the body of Christ." Therefore, churches ought to, at the very least, exist in order to equip the people of the Body of Christ with the result that the Body is built up (or matured; as opposed to numerical growth) for the glory of God (Doxological focus).[117]

Social transformation can be part of the "sphere of influence" of a godly leader who can motivate and mobilize others for holistic ministry/missions as defined in the following:

Christians motivated by their love for God and neighbors (within or without one's socio-cultural context) mobilized to be engaged in multi-dimensional services to Him by serving others, inclusively caring for the spiritual, psychological, social, physical, etc. well beings of others with multi-facet services (religious & charity, public & private, etc.) and at multi-levels (personal and institutional, local and global), in the framework of reconciliation vertically with God, horizontally with humanity and hierarchically with the created order.[118]

The sphere of influence can also be extended to have transformational impact in the marketplace. Details of such an approach can be found in the book – Enoch Wan and Howard Shauhau Chen. *Marketplace Transformation: Motivating and Mobilizing Chinese Churches in the Silicon Valley for Gospel Transformation*.[119]

Summary

Section 3 is concluded by this chapter on "becoming" in intercultural leadership. The narrative of "becoming" in the practice of intercultural leadership has been provided in this chapter as the final phase of the process of transformational change for growth. In addition to the lineal/processual narrative, we have added the idea of multi-layer (synchronic) description to complement the diachronic description of transformational growth in intercultural leadership. This chapter is also an attempt to provide an answer to the question: what influence do leader and follower(s) have on each other and beyond, leading to transformational growth?

---

[117] Enoch Wan and Jace Cloud, *Doxological Missiology: Theory, Motivation, and Practice*, 93.
[118] Wan, "Mission Amid Global Crisis: Holistic Mission to Diaspora Groups."
[119] Enoch Wan and Howard Chen, *Marketplace Transformation*.

SECTION 3

TRANSFORMATIONAL GROWTH: INTERCULTURAL DISCIPLESHIP

CHAPTER 8
Intercultural Discipleship Introduction

Defining Discipleship

This book is about leadership, discipleship and mentoring in terms of relational transformation. This particular section will consider the topic of discipleship and disciple-making. In light of that topic, the definition of what we mean by "discipleship" is presented in relational terms:

- Relational discipleship is a 2-step process (within the context of the convergence between the Triune God and the Christian community) by which a non-Christian (a) firstly being born again by the Holy Spirit, then (b) becoming a faithful follower of Christ in total submission to His lordship as required by Christ and prescribed by the Scriptures, walking in the Holy Spirit (vertically) with fruitfulness, taking up his/her cross {denying himself/herself} and forsaking all (horizontally). (Mt 10:37-38; 16-24; Mk 8:34; Lk 14:26-27,33).

Of course, just as people can grow in godliness, we also know that it is possible to go "from bad to worse." (2 Tim 3:13). When change is movement away from godliness, it is transgressive change. This is defined as "change caused by the dynamism from the enemy of the Triune God and by nature that is contrary to the attributes of God and His will, His revelation in Jesus Christ and in the Scripture -the opposite of "transformational change."[120]

In this discipleship section we will focus on the positive transformational backgrounds to the idea of human change and will not deeply consider that transgressive side to human change.

Matthew 28:18 -20 is one of the most frequently cited Biblical passages that speaks of discipleship. Those last words prior to the Lord's ascension into heaven highlight four important principles of Christian discipleship:

1) Discipleship is by nature transcultural, intended to extend into all the world. This is further seen in John's visions in the Book of the Revelation where he tells us that those from every nation, tribe, people and tongue will worship the Lord around His throne (Rev 5:9 and 7:9).

---

[120] Wan and Raibley, *Transformational Change in Christian Ministry*, 7.

2) Discipleship is designed for people to teach one another. If you are a disciple, you are called to make disciples. This principle is again seen in 2 Timothy 2:2 where Paul calls on his own disciple (Timothy) to entrust what he had received to other faithful people.
3) Discipleship is based on the Word of God. It is not a simple matter of sharing human insights or wisdom, but discipleship is tied integrally to "teaching them to observe all that I have commanded."
4) Discipleship is intensely vertical as well as horizontal. The Lord's promise "to be with you" points to the vertical reality that as we go about the human side of making disciples, we do so in reliance and obedience to the presence and guidance that we receive from our Lord.

Through the remainder of this section, these four principles will stand as Biblical witness to help us form a Scripturally accurate view of discipleship.

There is one other important introductory principle: making disciples can be done individually, and it can also be corporate. The Church, in its healthiest form, is a gathering of disciples. Acts 6:7 is just one of many verses that speak of the disciples who came to believe in Jesus after His death, burial, resurrection and ascension. Those disciples gathered together with the apostles who focused on prayer and the ministry of the Word (Acts 6:4). The point here is that congregational teaching is legitimately one form of discipleship.

Looking at these definitions of relational discipleship, there are three levels of transformation mentioned in that definition:

- the transformation that brings one into the new life in Christ, which leads to increased understanding of Christian truth, and
- the transformation that takes place as a believer applies truth in humility, in service, in fruitfulness, in self-denial.
- The transformation that takes place as a group of believers (the *ecclesia*) are being changed and transformed together.

Discipleship in Terms of Transformational Interaction

The figure below describes how relationship applies to discipleship. The importance of Being, Belonging and Becoming as applied to discipleship will become clearer as we consider each one in detail.

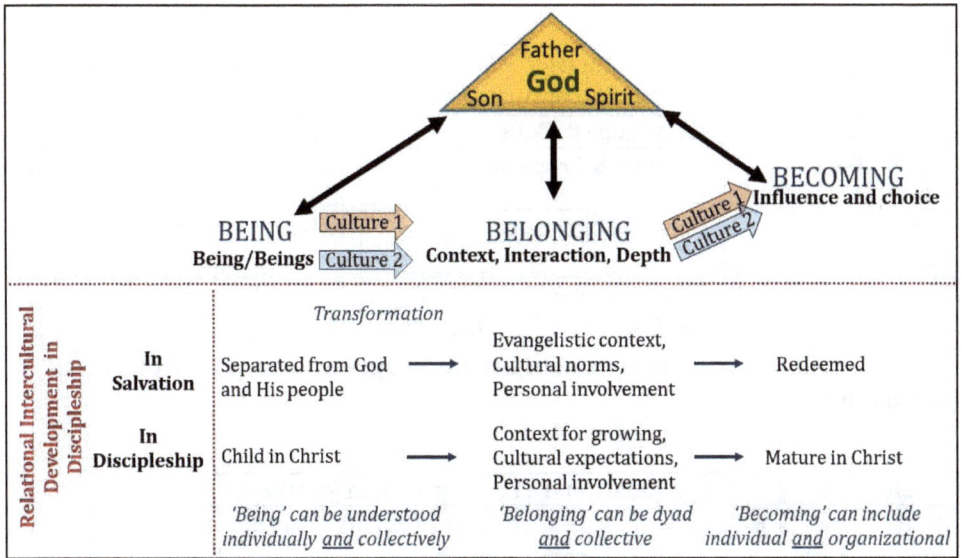

Figure 8-1. Relational Intercultural Development in Discipleship

It is important to realize what this diagram is NOT saying. Humanistic and rationalistic educational paradigms are built on mechanistic, methodological, managerial approaches to education. It is as if the key to education is simply to have the right outline and teaching methods.

Relational Discipleship, on the other hand, leads to an understanding of discipleship that is not mechanistic or managerial, but rather is based on the reality of vertical and horizontal relationships. Figures 8-1 and 8-2 demonstrate the differences between managerial and relational approaches to training in general and to discipleship in particular.

Approach / Level	Programmatic/ Managerial/ Entrepreneur	Relational Discipleship & Pastoral
(Discipleship) Individual — Goal	Knowledge & Skills	Personal relationship
Focus	Program & Procedure	Personal beings/Beings interacting
Strategy	Event & Formulaic	Relationship: 1st Vertical + 2nd Horizontal
Preference	Quantitative & measurable goals: Bigger is better	Qualitative & Relation-oriented

Figure 8-2. Comparing Discipleship from Programmatic and Relational Approaches[121]

Element	Jesus' Relational Training seen in Matthew's Gospel
What to be achieved	Followers of the Leader who are willing to lay down their lives for His Kingdom mission
Focus	Character formation with a heavy emphasis on humility and right relationships
Strategy	Invites people to follow, teaches didactically, occasionally and through example
Success/ Evaluation	Obedience (7:24-27), Perseverance (10) Anti-success: miracle workers (7:21-23), "great ones" (20:25), contemporary religious leaders (23)

Figure 8-3. Jesus' Relational Training in Matthew's Gospel[122]

Even recognizing that humanistic and rationalistic education is increasingly aware of relational patterns, that understanding of "relational" is limited to the horizontal relationship between people ("horizontal relationships").The people involved can only be described in psychological-socio-economic-political terms. The Belonging that might create interactions between people are limited to human cultures, human contexts, and human interactions. Likewise, relational patterns that are limited to horizontal terms can only discuss outcomes in the limited sphere of skills, knowledge and/or attitudes that can be measured and observed.

Refer to Figure 2-4, Multi-level, Multi-dimensional and Multi-stage of Relationship.[123]

---

[121] Robert Penner, "Kingdom Citizens on Mission: A Missiological Reading of Matthew's Gospel for Missionary Preparation" (Portland, OR, Western Seminary, 2017), 86.

[122] Based on Penner, 86.

[123] Adapted from Wan, "The Paradigm of Relational Realism," 3.

Relational Transformation Paradigm

In terms of Christian discipleship, the limitations of that flat world of purely human, methodological interaction is far short of the richness of "new life in Christ" which is "abundant and eternal." The following figure compares popular and relational approaches to training.

Element	Popular	Relational
What to be achieved	Skills, knowledge, etc.	Spiritual authority
Focus	Program and process	People
Strategy	Traditional	Interactive and andragogic
Success/ Evaluation	Measurable outcome	Non-linear, but holistic
What to be achieved	A proficient leader with followers; leaving a legacy	An exemplary follower of Christ who inspires others
Focus	Making a leader according to prevailing cultural norms; success and authority	Cultivating a leader according to the Kingdom of God – one who shares God's love with others. Authority is based on humility (character) and mutuality (relationship)
Strategy	Leadership training material from various paradigms and various means; content based	Teaching content in the context of relationships
Success/ Evaluation	Popular context: gain votes	Faithfulness and fruitfulness

Figure 8-4. Comparing Leadership Paradigms: Popular vs Relational[124]

This figure will guide us into a view of discipleship that is multifaceted and multidimensional, built on the headings of Being, Belonging and Becoming. As we consider disciple-making and discipleship, our discussion will include conceptual description, examples and conclusions. Many examples will be drawn from the classic work on discipleship written by A. B. Bruce, *The Training of the Twelve*.[125]

---

[124] Wan and Chen, *Marketplace Transformation*, 19.

[125] A. B. Bruce, *The Training of the Twelve: How Jesus Christ Found and Taught the 12 Apostles; A Book of New Testament Biography*, Second edition (Grand Rapids: Christian Classics Ethereal Library), accessed January 9, 2023, https://www.nobts.edu/discipleship/downloadable-documents1/leadership-folder/The%20Trainin%20of%20the%20Twelve.pdf.

CHAPTER 9
Being in Intercultural Discipleship
(Considers the question, "Who all are involved in Discipleship?")

Relational discipleship is a form of transformational change that takes place through the interactions of Father, Son, Spirit, people, angelic beings, and/or demonic beings. Relational Intercultural Discipleship speaks of the interactions between those Beings (Triune God) and beings (created beings) toward positive growth in godly character when coming from different human cultures. In that way, relational discipleship contrasts with transgressional development where influences and choices lead to an ungodly approach to life.

The kinds of growth and change that can happen within vertical relationships are different from the changes that take place in the horizontal realm. The following figure shows how education in purely horizontal terms leads to the well-known educational goals of knowledge, attitude and skill. In the vertical realm, though, growth is seen in faith, hope and love. Both the horizontal and the vertical speak of three dimensions. The potential growth for horizontal change is very restricted in comparison to the potential growth that comes from vertical relational transformation.

Dimension	Transformative Change		
	Faith	**Love**	**Hope**
Vertical (God working in us)	1. Receptive of God's Word & work: salvation & illumination 2. Gain understanding of major themes, genres, & teachings of the Bible	1. Loyal to lordship of Christ as disciple 2. Abide in Him, passion for Him & His will	1. The fruit of the Spirit & walk in the Spirit (Gal. 4) 2. Kingdom-orientation & eternal perspective
	Cognitive: Knowing	**Attitudinal: Willing**	**Practical: Doing**
Horizontal (God working through us)	1. Practice God's truth in lifestyle and servanthood. 2. Member of faith-community: Koinonia & ecclesia	1. Channeling the love of God to others; mutuality & reciprocity, allelon "one and other" 2. Practice the Great Commandment & fulfill the Great Commission	1. Successfully attend and participate in church and its ministries 2. Exercise spiritual gifts to serve others 3. Be an agent of transformative change

Figure 9-1. Relational Training for Transformative Change: Dimensions & Aspects[126]

When we think of the Relational Beings of the Trinity, we see three who are distinct and yet One. The Father is not the Son nor the Spirit; they are different Beings in their own right. Similarly, humans have distinct personalities, levels of physical ability, levels of intellectual ability, etc. In the realm of created spirits (angels and demons) there are unique traits that characterize one angel as opposed to another, or one demon in distinction to another. Deuteronomy 6:4 tells us God is One even as New Testament passages distinguish Father, Son, and Spirit.

The following three figures illustrate some of the variables which distinguish human individuals from one another.

---

[126] Wan and Chen, *Marketplace Transformation: Motivating and Mobilizing Chinese Churches in the Silicon Valley for Gospel Transformation.*, 19.

Variables Between Human Beings
Male/female
Age
Physical attributes: size, health, right/left handed
Learning style: reflexive, concrete, abstract, active
Musical or artistic ability
Personality traits
Emotional attributes focus: emotions as "between us" or "within me"
Social rank
Profession
Teaching style (especially of the Disciple-Maker)
Spiritual life: there is a difference between people who are Spiritually born again and those who are not
Relational preference: with whom, in what kind of relational patterns is the person most comfortable?
Literate preference (written) or narrative preference (orality)

Figure 9-2. Examples of Some Variables that Distinguish Humans from One Another[127]

Variables Between Angel/demon Beings
Angel or demon as beginning distinction
Roles held in the spirit world vary

Figure 9-3. Variables that Distinguish Created Spirit Beings

Variables Between Divine Beings
Father is distinct from Son, and both are distinct from Spirit
All are God
Difference in roles
The Son shares human physical life and death

Figure 9-4. Variables that Distinguish One Member of Triune God from Others

Thinking of the implications for relational discipleship, these levels of variation in both the Creator Beings and created beings leads to important implications for discipleship. Our definition of discipleship includes the process of receiving eternal life and growing toward maturity. Both of those steps happen in a beautiful cooperation where Triune God brings about the growth

---

[127] For a discussion of 'between us' and 'within us' emotions, see Batja Mesquita, *Between Us: How Cultures Create Emotions* (New York, NY: W. W. Norton & Company, 2022).

and yet He calls humans to active involvement in teaching one another. With such a wide variety of individual characteristics, the process of making disciples includes:

1. <u>Flexibility in methods depending on age</u>. Content and process must be appropriate for the learner. A child can be discipled (Deut. 6, Josh. 24:15, 2 Tim. 1:5 as just a few examples). Children, though, learn and grow differently than adults, calling for flexibility in methods.

The figure below shows an interesting reality when it comes to ages: the cultural patterns within an age cohort have a big impact on how discipleship is understood and practiced. Looking at recent generations in the U.S., the Boomer generation has the lowest total involvement in disciple-making, while Gen Z shows the highest levels of people who are involved in discipleship. It is clear that ages and the expectations within a generation all have profound implications on discipleship.

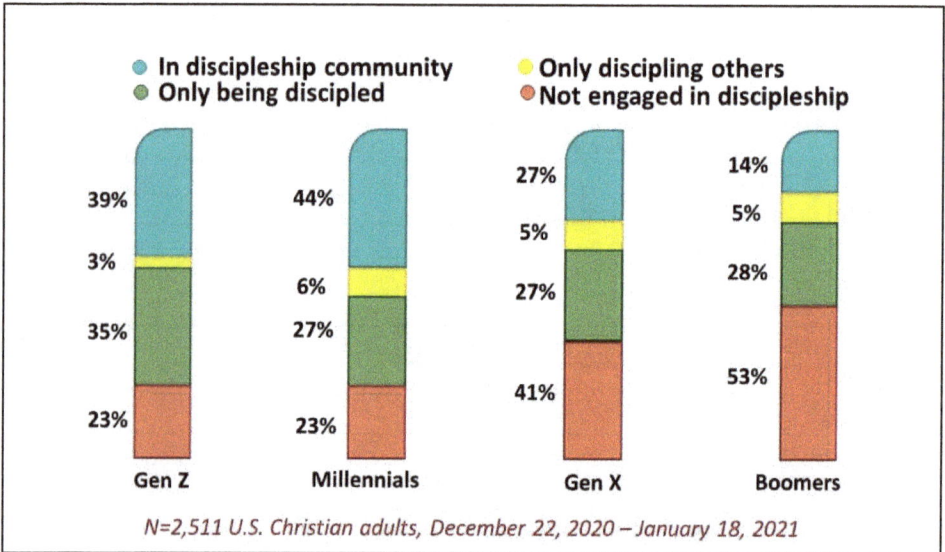

Figure 9-5. Discipleship Community, by Generation[128]

2. <u>Flexibility in methods for adults, depending on life circumstance</u>. Paul, for example, gives instruction in dealing with older men differently than younger men (1 Tim 5:1). That chapter later points to individualized treatment of widows as compared to younger, married women (1 Tim 5).

---

[128] *Growing Together: A Three-Part Guide for Following Jesus and Bringing Friends on the Journey* (The Barna Group, 2022), 23.

3. Flexibility depending on personal traits like intelligence, artistic inclinations, and emotional health. A person who has significant social difficulties would be discipled differently from someone who is skilled in social relationships. Similarly, highly literate people would be discipled differently than someone with a strong preference for oral learning.

4. Jude calls for discernment about the people we draw close to, shaping our involvement with those who are unbelievers. He makes a distinction between mockers (Jude 18), doubters (v. 22) and those who can be "snatched from the fire" (v. 23). Those differences call for different methods of teaching and involvement: some call us to renew our own faith lest we are led astray; others call us to mercy, and still others call us to act with haste, as if snatching a victim out of a fire.

5. Another important implication of the variability between Beings and beings is the importance of maintaining the vertical relationships even as we seek to make disciples in horizontal terms. Acts 16:14 is one of many verses that speak to the fact that human teaching is essential but cannot bear fruit without the work of the Spirit of God.

Jesus was aware of the individual characteristics of those He called to be disciples. Bruce points out that Jesus Himself called each of the twelve (John 6:70), knowing that one would betray Him. Jesus purposefully called both the Publican Matthew and the Zealot Simon. Bruce calls us to appreciate the way that Jesus deliberately discipled people from a variety of backgrounds:

> It gives one a pleasant surprise to think of Simon the zealot and Matthew the publican, men coming from so opposite quarters, meeting together in close fellowship in the little band of twelve. In the persons of these two disciples extremes meet - the tax-gatherer and the tax-hater: the unpatriotic Jew, who degraded himself by becoming a servant of the alien ruler; and the Jewish patriot, who chafed under the foreign yoke and sighed for emancipation. The union of opposites was not accidental, but was designed by Jesus as a prophecy of the future. He wished the twelve to be the church in miniature or germ; and therefore He chose them so as to intimate that, as among them distinctions of publican and zealot were unknown so in the church of the future there should be neither Greek nor Jew, circumcision nor uncircumcision, bond nor free, but only Christ - all to each and in each of the all.[129]

Relational discipleship is not a "one size fits all" methodology. It begins with the realization that there are real differences between people. Discipling

---

[129] Bruce, *The Training of the Twelve*, 32.

encourages growth. Methods that help one person mature might be quite different from the methods that work well for another person.

Some years ago, a former co-worker launched a new ministry. In his role as a young leader, he asked if I would meet on occasion to disciple in terms of leadership. I was honored by the request, and immediately started thinking about what I could do to lead those conversations. As this was a new sort of discipleship for me, I decided to use an approach that a former leader had used with me decades before. I chose a book that would give us leadership content and also facilitate conversation on a variety of topics.

My problem was that I didn't consider the personality and learning styles of this new relationship! In fact, we only discussed one chapter in the book, and even that was a very short and strained conversation. As I think back, my decision to use material that had been influential in my own life was rooted in the wrong question. The question I was asking was "how can I disciple this person?" – putting the emphasis on my own perspectives and experience. A much better question would have been, "what is the best learning approach for the person who has asked for this discussion? How can I shape my experiences for the best impact in this young leader?" When we consider the importance of individual characteristics in the realm of discipleship, we become learner-centric in our approach. My failed attempt at discipling in leadership, on the other hand, was curriculum and teacher-centric.

Relational discipleship starts by recognizing the individual characteristics of the Beings/beings who are involved. Rather than fall back to the methods that were effective in our own lives, or to the newest books and materials in our own people groups, we do well to start with a desire to understand the actual people with whom we are interacting. That approach to discipleship is aware of the person as an individual and as a member of a culture.

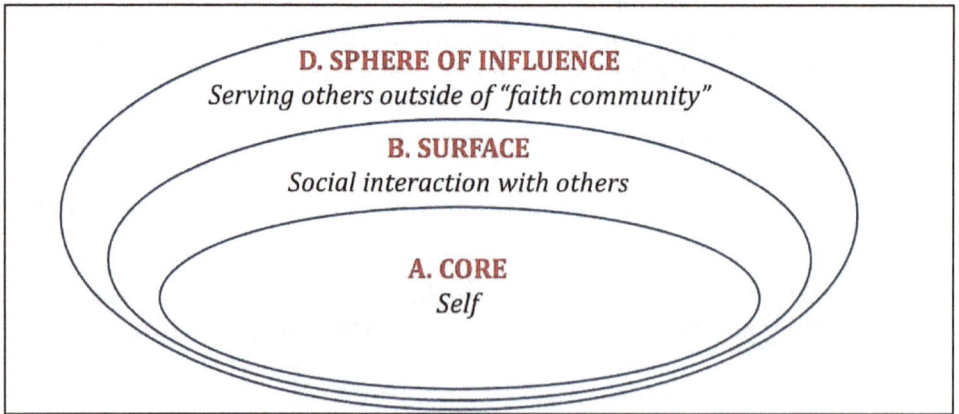

D. SPHERE OF INFLUENCE
Serving others outside of "faith community"

B. SURFACE
Social interaction with others

A. CORE
Self

Figure 9-6. Multi-layers of Intercultural Discipleship

When we consider discipleship as a process, Figure 5-1, repeated here (9-6), is a starting point. Just as multilayer analysis can help conceptualize leadership it also helps conceptualize discipleship. The three levels of core, surface, and spheres of influence can be described for both the one discipling (Discipler) and the one being discipled (Disciple).

Those two descriptions begin in two separate, distinct, unrelated individuals. Those two unrelated people, represented as two unrelated and distinct circles, each have their own sets of strengths, weaknesses, likes, dislikes, spheres of influence, personality traits, and habits of social interaction.

In the next chapter we will see how life-interaction draws those two independent circles closer, forming a relationship. The movement from independent circles to inter-related circles occurs over time (diachronic) and illustrates the process of relational transformational discipleship.

Life circumstances are also relevant to the question of "who is involved in a discipling relationship." In the last few pages we spoke about personal characteristics of the people involved. Now, we want to consider their life situations.

We particularly look at transition points: those "gray areas" where a person is shifting from one circumstance to another. Jack Mezirow has written in horizontal terms of these transition points, calling them "Disruptive Dilemmas."[130] These are moments that are especially apt opportunities for discipleship toward godly maturity.

In Christian discipleship, we want to see these transition points both in horizontal and in vertical terms. To see God at work across the panorama of one's life is a powerful lesson on the greatness of God and on the power of His relational interactions with His children.

Some of those moments of life transition are listed, together with discipleship suggestions, in Figure 9-7.

---

[130] Jack Mezirow, *Learning as Transformation.*

Human Transition	Horizontal Characteristics	Vertical Insights and Growth Opportunity
From non-believer to believer	Newborn in Christ	Teach the essentials of the faith *
From non-church to involved in church	Learning the culture of a local assembly	Teaching to do all things "decently and in order" and "above all things to put on love"
From single to newlywed	Establishing a strong faith-based foundation for the new married couple	To learn God's intention for marriage as expressed in the Bible
Birth of children	Child-rearing in a faith-based environment	Rather than raising children with the philosophies of the world, this lets us focus on raising children in the fear and admonition of the Lord
Entering midlife	Developing a new mind for mature service	"Putting away childish things" – there can be deliberate relational interaction to model and to teach about increasing maturity in the church.
Losing a spouse	From married to widow/widower	Dealing with grief, and moving ahead into a new phase of life with changing social relationships.
Moving into old age	There are cultures where people anticipate and rejoice to age. Other cultures try to avoid aging and wish to live forever young.	Seeing the natural process of aging as part of the plan of a wise God, and making the most of the relational opportunities that arise with age.

*in many traditions and works on discipleship, this is the only part of life that is considered as part of the discipleship curricula.

Figure 9-7. Life Transitions and Related Discipleship Opportunities.

It is important to recall that life transitions are celebrated and recognized in different ways across cultures. Moon[131] reminds us of the importance of cultural expressions like ceremony, symbol, proverb, and dance for passing on a worldview from one generation to another. Often the ceremonies mark important life transitions (the marriage ceremony marks transition from single to wed, for instance). One culture's normal expressions of transition may not be shared by other cultures, and so the intercultural disciple-maker needs to pay special attention to the cultural habits surrounding transitions.

Moon's powerful reminder is based on the equally powerful work of Paul Hiebert.[132] Hiebert's conclusion is that discipleship, at its root, is a transformation of worldview from that which is commonly held in a community to a biblical, Christian worldview[133]. Such a transition is a life-long process for a person; one with ups and downs at that. The massive transformation that is needed to move from a world-centered worldview to a Kingdom of God centered worldview is exactly why the vertical component is absolutely essential. "Unless one is born again, he cannot see the Kingdom of God," said Jesus (John 3:3).

In a similar way to the life transitions, there are also community-wide transitions. Part of discipleship is to teach and prepare a Christian community for the retirement of a beloved pastor, or for the arrival of a new pastor. Communities also can be discipled toward growth in times of grief (the death of a key member), upheaval (political or military interventions in the nation), and disasters (tornados, pandemics). Community transitions, in other words, bring opportunities for discipleship growth, both at the individual and at the group level.

Yet another way that community "being" is important to consider in discipling is in terms of international migration. Consider, for example, a church pastor from East Africa serving a congregation located in the US State of New Jersey. There are cultural connections, but now everyone is in a life-style transition of learning to live as an expat outside of their homeland.

Compare that to an American pastor serving that same East African community. The knowledge of how to weep with those who weep, or how to teach within the cultural preferences of the people, are going to be quite different between that US pastor and the East African congregation.

Both of those two circumstances would be quite different from an East African pastor serving a congregation in his homeland.

---

[131] W. Jay Moon, *Intercultural Discipleship: Learning from Global Approaches to Spiritual Formation* (Grand Rapids, Michigan: Baker Academic, 2017), 53.

[132] Hiebert, *Transforming Worldviews*, 307-326.

[133] Hiebert, *Transforming Worldviews*, 332-333.

The point is that, when we consider the "being" part of discipleship, there are community as well as individual elements to the discussion. Those community patterns can be affected by many issues, including the national origins of a people and their cultural expectations.

Conclusions: The Role of Being in Discipleship

Discipleship is the form of specialized education that fosters Christian growth toward maturity, both individually and in community. That deep discipleship can occur across all of life but is particularly powerful in those moments of disruption at a personal or community level.

In this chapter, we have seen that Relational Discipleship calls the Christian worker to:

- Discernment to understand the characteristics of those who are being discipled.
- Flexibility of methods to best meet the needs of disciples.
- An enduring dependence on the Lord Himself to guide the discipleship and to open hearts to new approaches and concepts.
- Openness to disciple people from a variety of backgrounds -following the example of Jesus whose disciples included political and social diversity.
- Awareness of the potential for growth that comes at times of personal transition.
- Awareness of the potential for growth that comes during times of community transition.

CHAPTER 10
Belonging in Intercultural Discipleship

Belonging in Discipleship

The Bible speaks of the Church as "The Body of Christ." That metaphor leads to at least two strong relational thoughts:

1   The Body is made of multiple, varied parts. Those parts are united into one Body, but they are also diverse in their forms and uses. (1 Cor. 12:12 ff). Relationship, in other words, is woven into the very nature of the horizontal humanity of the Church.
2   The Body of Christ is meant for relationship with the Head of the Church, Jesus Himself. Relationship, in other words, is woven into the very nature of the vertical interaction between Triune God and the members of His church.

How do vertical and horizontal relationships effect growth to spiritual maturity? That kind of growth is at the root of our definition of discipleship, and so it is important for us to consider this question.

The starting point is to consider what Jesus taught: to love God and to love others (Matthew 22:37-40, John 13:35-36) It seems axiomatic but true nonetheless that vertical and horizontal love takes place in community, not in isolation. There are certainly times and situations that call for private prayer and reflection. But those private minutes are a sort of abstinence of community which points to the normative reality that spiritual growth happens in relationship. Relationship with God and with other people takes place in community. Discipleship is a transformative process of vertical and horizontal growth.

In this section we will follow Wan and Kim's relational elements to see how belonging feeds into discipleship. Their analysis leads to the realization that relationship is not a simple concept. There are variations in what makes for a healthy relationship, depending on five variables: the nature of the Beings/beings, the context of the relationship, the interactions that become part of the relationship, the depth of relationship and the influence or outcomes that grow from the relationship.[134]

---

[134] Enoch Wan and Natalie Kim, *Relational Intercultural Training for Practitioners of Business As Mission: Theory and Practice* (Western Academic Publishers, 2022), 76-78.

Belonging in Context: Culture

The first way to understand "belonging" is in terms of culture. A working definition is that culture refers to the patterns that a group of people consider to be normal and acceptable. It is a sort of group habit that affects thought, emotions, daily activities, the raising of children, relationships between people, and even the norms of relating to God and to Spirit beings. What's more, practically speaking, those cultural patterns are invisible to those who live within its patterns. They reflect real pressures to conform to group norms but they can be hard to identify simply because often those are the only norms a person has ever considered. We grow up aware of certain life patterns and can hardly imagine other ways of living.

Those cultural patterns of our group, then, are the context of belonging in which we as people live.

But since the Fall of man in Genesis 3 we have the problem expressed by Isaiah: "Woe is me! I am a man of unclean lips and I live among a people of unclean lips" (Isaiah 6:5). We are individually and collectively estranged from God. The group to which we belong will lead us astray from the God we wish to know and serve. Yet, in Christ we are "in the world but not of the world." (John 17: 14, 15). The closer that we make our "belonging" to be with the world, the less we are shaped by Christ.

The importance of belonging within the community of the Kingdom of God becomes evident in that light. Our context inevitably shapes our behaviors, our thinking, our attitudes. We can easily see the danger of living solely in the community of people who have no vertical relationship. We can see how belonging to the world will move us away from closeness with God. As James puts it, "friendship with the world is enmity with God" (James 4:4).

The church universal (*ecclesia*) is the Kingdom community to which God's people rightly belong. "So then you are no longer strangers and aliens but you are fellow citizens with the saints, and are of God's household, having been built upon the foundation of the apostles and prophets, Christ Jesus Himself being the corner stone in whom the whole building, being fitted together is growing into a holy temple in the Lord in whom you also are being built together into a dwelling of God in the Spirit." (Ephesians 2: 19-21).

Greg Ogden's work, *Transforming Discipleship*, proposes the use of small group as a context for making full-life disciples in the context of the US church. Based on the relationships in which Jesus and Paul made disciples, he offers a pattern of reproducing small groups that meet for a prescribed amount of time, later to be disbanded so that each member of a small group begins to lead a new group.[135]

In Ogden's approach, the community that will be effective at making disciples will be marked by[136]

>Trust
>Bible focus
>Mutual accountability
>Practical outworking

Evelyn and Richard Hibbert take the idea of disciple-making communities into the realm of missions methods. They also present the idea of belonging within small groups as a discipleship context. They envision those small groups as a tool that in some cases will multiply other small groups. Belonging within discipleship contexts, in other words, can become a means for evangelism especially in situations that do not permit the establishment of traditional churches.[137]

Whether we consider it in terms of Ogden's model or a different form, at any rate, discipleship is growth that happens within the community of Christians that we call "*ecclesia.*" In that community we learn to live in the world but not of the same essence as the world.

In terms of belonging to the world, there are many practices in the world that are not contrary to our relationship with God. These are areas that we can practice as we live in the context of belonging to family, to society, and to our local communities. "If it is possible, as far as it depends on you, live at peace with everyone" (Romans 12:8) is one of many exhortations to be at peace with the earthly communities we belong to.

We ultimately belong, though, to another Kingdom, and it is in that context of belonging to the Church that we grow in discipleship. Understanding and submitting to the Word, prayer, joining together in worship, and serving one another are all areas that rightly are part of the discipleship we find in the local and universal church. In some parts of the world, there is open animosity between the kingdom of this world and the Kingdom of God. It is in the Kingdom community that we learn to suffer and feel rejection for the sake of our Savior. In other places, the Kingdom of God and the kingdom of this world live quietly next to each other. In either case, they are two distinct cultures -

---

[135] Greg Ogden, *Transforming Discipleship: Making Disciples a Few at a Time*, Revised and Expanded (Downers Grove, IL: IVP Books, 2016).

[136] Ogden, 144 - 163

[137] Evelyn Hibbert and Richard Hibbert, *Walking Together On The Jesus Road: Intercultural Discipling* (Littleton, CO: William Carey Library, 2018).

two distinct patterns of life. In either case there are moments that call on us to forsake the world and cling to the Savior. In either case we belong to Christ's Kingdom and we learn, through the community, to stay faithful even in difficult moments. The community of God's people that brings us such encouragement and teaching is the community we call the church.

The importance of belonging to Christ's Kingdom and thus being strangers and pilgrims in the world cannot be stressed too much. As Enoch Wan and John Jay Flinn state in their description of US life, ". . . post-Christian formation has infiltrated the church to the extent that the Christian worldview often bears little visible difference to that of the overriding cultural worldview."[138] One of the strongest tools to bring Christianity into the marketplace of US life is a Community that is at once a witness and an encouragement to its individual members who are trying to live as salt and light in a post-Christian context.

Belonging in Context: The Community's Role when we Suffer

James exhorts us to count it all joy when we encounter various trials (James 1:2) because those trials display the direction of our inner inclinations. Under pressure, will we move closer to the world? Or will we move closer to the Kingdom of God? When we face difficulties, will we seek the short-term gain and immediate relief that the world pretends to offer? Or will we trust that our God is working all things out for our good? (Romans 8:8). If we have a choice in moving toward the Kingdom or toward the world under normal circumstances, we have that temptation even more so when we have a problem that can apparently be solved by moving toward the world. Which will we choose to belong to? James reminds us that trials show us the ultimate inclination of our hearts. It is by belonging to the community of the Kingdom that we find encouragement, compassion, and comfort for moments of difficulty. Ephesians 4:32 calls those who belong in the Kingdom community to be kind to one another, tender hearted, forgiving.

Because we belong to a community in Christ we grow through the encouragement, the teaching, the example, and the comfort that we find in the Body of Christ.

---

[138] Enoch Wan and John Jay Flinn, *Holistic Mission through Mission Partnership: An Instrumental Case Study in La Ceiba, Honduras* (Western Academic Publishers, 2021), 25.

Belonging in Context: Intercultural Relationships

Relational Patterns across Cultures.

Intercultural ministry calls us to deliberately leave the patterns (culture) we grew up with for the sake of extending the Lord's Kingdom to which we belong. In ministry among a culture that is different from one's own, we learn to leave even what is "good" from our home patterns so that we can better proclaim the excellencies of our King and our Lord to a people different than our own.

Intercultural studies in general and missions study in particular call attention to patterns of life that differ from culture to culture. People involved in cross-cultural or intercultural ministry will have to navigate new patterns of life around themes such as:[139]

- Patterns that show how the group and the individual should appropriately interact (Individualism/Collectivism).
- Patterns of how a leader interacts with his/her people (High/Low Power distance)
- Patterns of valuing one form of work and production over others in the community (Masculine or Feminine cultures).
- Patterns of valuing strict self-discipline on one hand, compared to patterns that encourage indulgence.
- Patterns of motivation in support of culturally appropriate behaviors: are we motivated by obedience to a rule or law, by adherence to social norms that bring honor to us and our families, or is the motivation to avoid supernatural confrontations by use of powerful magic? (Honor/Shame, Guilt/Innocence, Power/Fear).
- Patterns of emotional interaction: are we motivated by emotions that we perceive as dwelling within us, or by emotions that grow between the people who are involved in relationship? (Are emotions "in us" or "between us?")[140]

These kinds of cultural variables show some of the variety found around the world. The intercultural gospel worker learns how to live within the patterns of

---

[139] For example, see contemporary intercultural literature such as:
- Hofstede, Geert, Gert Jan Hofstede, and Michael Minkov. *Cultures and Organizations: Software of the Mind, Third Edition.* 3 edition. New York: McGraw-Hill Education, 2010.
- Müller, Roland. *The Messenger, the Message, & the Community: Three Critical Issues for the Cross-Cultural Church Planter,* 2013.

[140] Batja Mesquita, *Between Us: How Cultures Create Emotions* (New York, NY: W. W. Norton & Company, 2022).

another group of people. When the missions world speaks of polycentric mission in the 21st century, we are talking about people from many parts of the world learning to live and minister with people in other parts of the world. Successful intercultural servants learn to leave even the innocent patterns of their own culture and instead recognize and adapt to the patterns of a new group of people for the purpose of announcing the Kingdom of God and pointing people to God's patterns.

Relational Patterns and Intercultural Teaching Methods

Thinking in terms of intercultural, polycentric discipleship, we also see the connection between belonging and teaching methods. The methods that a teacher uses and a group of learners prefers are both indications of their cultural expectations, their relational expectations, and their concept of what makes for good teaching.

As human beings we have individual preferences for how to learn. We discussed this earlier as part of the Being/being discussion of personal characteristics. Cultures also have long-standing patterns of what is considered to be good teaching and good learning. The methods that we use to make disciples are an important element of relational discipleship.

Craig Ott's 2022 publication *Teaching and Learning Across Cultures*[141] highlights educational differences related to concrete, abstract, holistic and analytical thought patterns. He delves into how worldview studies can help to shape the cross-cultural discipleship that is most appropriate for a given audience. He talks about social levels, group versus individual values, and the cultural preferences of which media is preferred for presenting a message.

Healthy and Unhealthy Relational Patterns in a Discipleship Context

Intercultural education and intercultural discipleship require us to think in terms of healthy intercultural relationships. The gospel messenger who is making disciples in an unfamiliar culture will do well to learn how teaching and learning are typically done in the new location, and to adjust his/her patterns to better fit in that new area.

As an example, in Western societies, we prefer individualism as a way for the person and the group to interact. We frequently speak of "one-on-one discipleship." In fact, there are many who would find that individual approach to be the only way they can imagine true discipleship.

But many other parts of the world would be uncomfortable with one-on-one methods. The idea of reading a book and then discussing it with one authority

---

[141] Ott, 2022.

or peer would be uncomfortable for these people. Discipleship as they know it includes group discussion, group experience, and group motivation.

I remember early in my ministry a time when I wanted to encourage the students and staff at a Latin American Bible Institute to have more robust times of reading the Bible and prayer. I suggested changing the daily schedule so that everyone spent more time in their quarters before starting the group activities of meals and classes. The response, from both students and staff, was a loud and serious, "NO!" My response was to ask why they didn't want to spend more time in the Bible and prayer. "No, *hermano* ... it is not that we don't want to have more time in the Bible and prayer. We just don't want to do that alone in our rooms."

I thought, again wrongly, that they were suggesting an organized preaching time where one person would lead the devotional time. "No, that is not it either, *hermano*. We like to read and pray individually. We just like to do that together." The final result was that we met in the dining room before breakfast for a time when each person could quietly read and pray - together in the same place, but not organized into an activity.

When we think of relational methods for discipleship, Jesus is our example. Looking through A. B. Bruce's study, we see how He spoke truth to His disciples (consider the Sermon on the Mount). He sent the disciples out to learn by doing. He gave them opportunities to watch Him perform miracles and answer questions. He asked them questions and then replied to their answers. He got involved in their discussions. In short, Jesus not only was aware of the different individual learning styles of His disciples; He also taught them according to the learning styles preferred by their cultures.

In fact, Jesus' teaching of the twelve included many other teaching methods. A. B. Bruce examines each of the following ways in which Jesus taught the disciples[142]:

- Calling them to observe
- Appealing to curiosity by teaching through parables
- Experience-based learning
- Confronting disbelief and animosity
- Prayer
- Comparing ritual with the heart of the ritual (true fasting)
- Evangelism - taking their message to unbelievers
- Sending them out to a limited audience before sending them to the world
- Testing of the heart and motivations (do you love Me for the food?)

---

[142] A. B. Bruce, *The Training of the Twelve: How Jesus Christ Found and Taught the 12 Apostles; A Book of New Testament Biography* (CreateSpace Independent Publishing Platform, 2018).

- Testing them in apparent danger (the storm on the sea. Jesus walking past)
- Slowly unveiling the purpose of His ministry and the reality of the cross
- Testing - who do people say I am? And who do you say I am?
- Plain speaking about His death only toward the end of their time together
- Forgiveness

There are some levels of Jesus' teaching that are not appropriate for us to provide, since we are finite created beings. And yet the truth is visible that Jesus' approach to shaping the lives of His disciples included a wide variety of concepts, experiences, and methods. He taught according to a sequence based on the readiness of His disciples and within the expectations of His culture.

Paul also exemplifies relational discipleship, especially in his relationship with Timothy. In *Relational Missionary Training*, we published a review of the life situations that Paul brought into his relational discipleship of Timothy:

- Cultural sensitivity
- Multicultural relationships
- Church growth
- Spiritual life in missionary outreach
- Evangelism and baptism in discipleship
- Recognition and reaction to demonic activity
- Responding to persecution
- Outreach strategy
- Missionary team formation
- Biblical knowledge[143]

Relationship Patterns and Domains of Education within Discipleship

When we make relational disciples in our own home culture we are often (not always!) intuitively aware of how to shape the interactions and the material to be well understood. That is probably not true when we move into another culture. To make disciples across cultures, educational efforts must actively engage at least the following domains:

- spiritual
- cognitive
- emotional

---

[143] Enoch Wan and Mark Hedinger, *Relational Missionary Training*, Urban Ministry in the 21st Century (Skycrest, CA: Urban Loft Publishers, 2017), 263–79.

- behavioral /skill
- social

How do we communicate that level of truth across cultural gaps? Being aware of content is only part of the picture. Presenting through a sense of belonging is also key.

Moon suggests that we learn to use the symbols, rituals, stories, proverbs, music, drama and dance of our host culture. He seeks worldview transformation toward Kingdom reality and truth by using the genres and forms of the host culture. Our entering into the communication patterns and features of a group of people is one avenue for building meaningful discipleship relationships[144].

It is important to see discipleship as using the communication patterns of the disciples. It is equally important to stress healthy relationship patterns between Discipler and Disciple. Another important area of interaction through teaching methods is how this topic is incorporated into the training of new missionaries.

Relationship Patterns in Discipleship of New Intercultural Gospel Workers

In the first place, new missionaries need to be encouraged to be flexible in their methods. This includes a motivation to change, if necessary, so that new disciples can learn and live biblical truths in familiar patterns of the learner, not necessarily of the teacher. Having a framework of alternative methods and being willing to use them is the key to this. It is doubtful if a new missionary can just memorize the best methods for making disciples before arrival. But a new missionary can be taught how to learn.[145] As they grow in understanding of how a people group learns and teaches, the cross-cultural disciple maker can also adjust their disciple-making to fit the learning/teaching norms of their hosts.

There is another important element in training missionaries related to teaching methods: discipleship is not aimed at helping people become like we are. We want to point to lifestyles and Christian behavior that model what the Scriptures tell us. This seems obvious, but in fact Christian workers across the centuries have struggled to separate their own cultural and personal lifestyle choices from the truths and exhortations of Scripture. As missionaries go "from

---

[144] Moon, 53.

[145] Mark Hedinger, *Culture Learning: The Art of Understanding What No One Can Teach You* (Portland, OR: CultureBound, 2021).

everywhere to everywhere" we see the tendency to teach people "follow my example." At first glance, that is brilliant! But with a bit of reflection we realize that very often our "example" is the adaptation of Christian truth to our own personal and cultural setting. It is much more complicated and yet also more effective to guide new Christians to grow in their understanding of the Bible and then to make disciples who follow Biblical patterns within their own cultural setting.[146]

The Hibberts add another important element to this "follow Jesus" model. If discipleship is formed around the habits of the human disciple-maker, then it leaves the new disciple in a very fragile situation when that more mature disciple-maker is unavailable. In an intercultural setting and especially in a missions setting, the disciple-maker will normally return home at some point. When the discipling is to follow Jesus, there is no disruption at the absence of the horizontal disciple-maker.

Relational Patterns and Emotions across Cultures

We have looked at Belonging as it applies to culture and as it applies to interaction with appropriate and recognizable teaching methods. We also belong to our groups based on the emotional ties that we experience.

Our emotional response to what and how we learn is an important part of discipleship. This can be seen by vocabulary that may, to some people, denote emotions (for example, "Jacob have I loved, and Esau have I hated" from Romans 9:13 quoting Malachi 1:1 - 3). This emotional response also grows from our cultural backgrounds. Author and researcher Batja Mesquita discusses how cultures create emotion. She compares cultures that see emotion as something inside a given person with cultures that see emotion as the response to a relationship between two or more people.[147]

Good discipleship will seek to understand how people in that community understand and apply the reality of emotions. At times those emotional foundations might be the same between the disciple and the disciple-maker. At times an older disciple-maker may need to adjust to the emotional language of a younger disciple. At any rate, we bear in mind that the interactions in a disciple-making relationship will include culture, methods, and emotions. The relational disciple-maker will be aware and will learn how to teach effectively with patterns of culture, teaching, and feeling that are comfortable and understandable to the disciples.

---

[146] Evelyn Hibbert and Richard Hibbert, *Walking Together On The Jesus Road: Intercultural Discipling* (Littleton, CO: William Carey Library, 2018), 195 and following.

[147] Mesquita, *Between Us*, 2022.

There is an especially important caution for the US missionary in this way. The US has a cultural habit of equating friendliness with healthy relationship; a concept not shared widely across the world.

This can be illustrated by a US missionary who misunderstands the word "friend," for instance, and assumes it to be based on emotional affinity. In those terms one might expect disciple/disciple-maker relationship to be always marked by positive, warm, affectionate feelings.

In many parts of the world, though, that would be inappropriate and even counter-productive for a discipleship relationship. That one means well and expects to produce healthy, positive effects is expected in all discipleship. But at times that positive result will include disagreeable tasks, and rebukes that might not feel "friendly" to the US gospel worker. An older pastor or missionary, for example, may actually be more effective by being a bit removed in demeanor - but the American missionary may misunderstand that apparent emotional distance as a negative. In fact, far from being negative, that emotional distance could be the most fruitful and appropriate way to shape discipleship relationships in some cases.

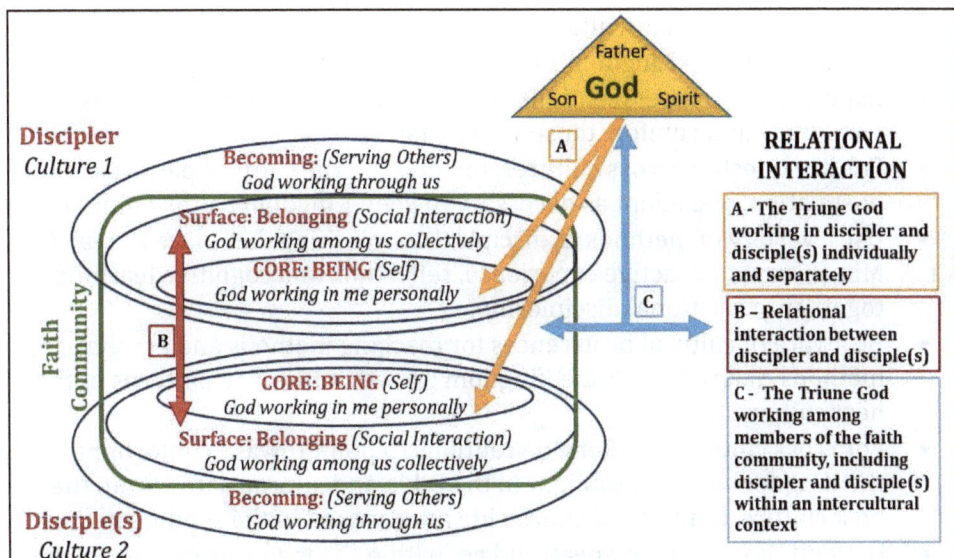

Figure 10-1. Intercultural Discipleship in Action

The connection between discipleship and belonging can be graphically described using the same diagram that was used in Figure 9-6, except now instead of a single, isolated figure there are two spheres in contact.

Figure 10-1 shows the interaction of two or more people from two cultures. Their interaction happens in the context of a faith community and in relationship with Triune God. Their core and surface interactions and sphere of influence interact with one another. It is important to note that all of the arrows have arrow heads on both ends; they are all two-way interactions.

The importance of that two-way relationship is that, on a horizontal plane, both the discipler and the disciple will be impacted by their interaction. In any healthy human relationship, both people will give and both will receive.

In the same way, God works in both the disciple-maker and the disciple. He brings growth and increasing maturity and the joy of His Spirit to all who are serving and growing.

God also receives from both the discipler and the disciple; He receives worship, honor, and glory from those who are growing in Him.

Conclusions

In this chapter on "Belonging" we have traced the importance of culture, teaching methods, and emotional ties within the relationships between disciple-maker and disciples. We have come to the following conclusions:

- Be at peace with secular culture as far as it is possible, but our goal is not to fit into the secular culture.
- Be conformed to Kingdom's cultural patterns and its values and truths.
- Expect trials and persecutions, and use our Christian relationships to encourage and comfort those who suffer.
- For discipleship across cultures, understand the cultural patterns of the host nation, and adapt as necessary to keep Kingdom truths in focus.
- Use a variety of methods to disciple. Discipleship takes place in real life. Mix observation, active experience, reflection, and cognitive learning together in relational discipleship.
- Be aware of cultural preferences for teaching methods and emphasize methods that will facilitate Kingdom growth within the patterns of the host culture.
- For cross cultural workers, be cautious to point toward conforming to the Kingdom of God as taught in the Bible and appropriate within the host culture, not toward church life as practiced in the sending nation.
- Understand, minister, speak and act within the language of emotion in the context of the host culture.
- For US people, be especially careful with the misappropriation of "friendliness." It is understood and practiced in the US quite differently than in most of the rest of the world.

CHAPTER 11
Becoming in Intercultural Discipleship

Our relational discipleship journey began with the characteristics that are true about a particular Divine Being or created being, and about the characteristics of communities that serve to foster discipleship. We then looked at belonging through the process of growth: how belonging affects teaching, cultural interactions, and emotional ties. Belonging within a group, in Christian terms, is so closely associated with "church" that we proposed the relational element of *ecclesia* as that whole-life environment where teaching and disciple-making can best occur.

We end with the goal of what we wish to see happen through relational discipleship. What is it that we want for a person or a community to become? What influence do we seek that will shape the person or people being discipled?

A Holistic Perspective on Discipleship Outcomes

In the first place, we have a holistic perspective of discipleship. "A most important goal for Christian education is to facilitate the transformation of students holistically - spiritually, relationally, cognitively, emotionally, and behaviorally (their lifestyles) - while preparing them for their work and ministry."[148]

Jesus modeled that same theme when He taught that a fully formed disciple will be like his teacher or master (Matt 10:24, Luke 6:40). This is an important corrective to discipleship programs that are limited to certain portions of human life. For years, discipleship was seen as an academic topic, with a goal of imparting knowledge. Later, there was a reaction to that cognitive approach that brought awareness of spiritual and behavioral growth through spiritual disciplines.

All of these areas are legitimately and properly part of relational discipleship, but for relational discipleship to live up to its calling it will weave together all of the realities of human interactions, both vertical and horizontal. The quote above speaks to that holistic perspective: relational discipleship seeks to influence growth toward Christian maturity in each disciple and within

---

[148] Ronald G. Hannaford, "A Model of Online Education Effecting Holistic Student Formation Appropriate for Global Cross-Cultural Contexts." (Los Angeles, Fuller Theological Seminary, 2012), 205.

the Community that is spiritual (vertical), relational (horizontal and social), cognitive, emotional and behavioral.

Domain	Outcomes for Individual Disciples	Outcomes for Communities of Disciples
Spiritual	Fruit of the Spirit; use of gifts to serve the Body; spiritual disciplines like prayer, Bible, etc. A vibrant walk with God in the Community of believers	Foster environment of prayer, Bible study, service, outreach A vibrant walk with God that is deliberate in corporately offering to Him worship, obedience, outreach, discipleship.
Relational	Social interactions that are culturally and spiritually appropriate for context	A Christian community that unites for spiritual growth, service, and outreach
Cognitive	Knowledge of Bible and Christian doctrines	Knowledge of Bible, knowledge of Christian doctrine and local church/denominational distinctives
Emotional	Self-control and ability to use emotions in ways that are relationally appropriate	Teaching cross-cultural differences in how emotion is understood and displayed
Behavioral	Wisdom in knowing appropriate actions for a Christian in given situations within given cultural settings	Harmony of interaction between members of the Christian community.

Figure 11-1. Holistic Outcomes for Discipleship

A Vague Announcement of Discipleship Outcomes

Reaching those holistic outcomes can be achieved in a number of ways. In the first place, relational discipleship that seeks holistic growth does not necessarily announce the details of its pathway at the outset. When Jesus began His ministry, He called people to be "fishers of men" (Matt 4: 19). To Nathanael, He promised, "you will see the heavens opened and the angels of God ascending and descending on the Son of Man" (John 1:51). Each of those was completely true and yet not detailed.

Contemporary pedagogy and andragogy both prefer specific, detailed previews of what will be taught. We are all accustomed to phrases like, "in this chapter you will learn .... " or "at the end of this activity, participants will have experienced and discussed .... ".

But the Master teacher gave a much looser preview: you will be fishers of men; you will see the angels of God ascending and descending on the Son of Man.

Jesus knew exactly where He would be leading in his discipleship of the Twelve. He was guiding them into full, abundant life (Matt 10:24 and Luke 6:40). He wanted the disciples to be with Him, to minister on His behalf and to learn from Him (Mark 3:13 - 19). But He did not say, "I am going to teach you a twelve point curriculum and at the end of the three years you will be able to teach, to do miracles, to heal. I am going to show you how to pray and to have fellowship with the Father. I am then going to enter into an intense time of teaching you what is My kingdom and what is the kingdom of this world. In that lesson I will be crucified and you will be scattered but don't worry - I will have discipled you sufficiently before that time so you can handle it and I will return to gather and instruct you again." He did not give that kind of detail upfront. I am glad for the sake of the Twelve, and I am just as glad that He hasn't chosen to tell me all that will be part of my journey. Vague previews can be much more powerful than detailed previews.

As one grows toward maturity in Christ, we begin to see reasons why it is better to give a brief preview of the purpose and outcomes of relational discipleship without going into much detail.

For one thing, too much detail can be confusing. Jesus' progressive relational discipleship grew from one stage to another. Some lessons were not appropriate for the novice disciples; time and experience were necessary. An announcement ahead of time could have discouraged the disciples by pointing to a reality they were not yet ready for.

The figure below uses the word, "process" in a number of places. Seeing the individual and institutional growth over time (diachronically) helps us to realize that relational discipleship is not an event but a process. Giving the appropriate lessons and experiences at the appropriate stage of development is more art than science, and is an important part of that relational discipleship process.

Recall Figure 4-5:

Approach / Level	Aspects	Popular ministry	Relationally transformational leadership
#1 – individual discipleship	Purpose	Knowledge, skills	Enriched relationships vertical + horizontal), spiritual maturity, God-honoring growth for Kingdom-purpose
	Focus	Program	People, process & relationships
	Strategy	Systematic transmission of knowledge & skills	Relational modeling & transformative process: God → leader → followers
	Evaluation	Quantifiable outcomes & numerical success	1st quality of spirituality & Kingdom-outcomes + 2nd institutional growth
#2 – institutional/Social	Purpose	Expansion of power, prestige & property	Enriched relationship, spiritual maturity, God-honoring accomplishments
	Focus	Program, enterprise & management efficiency	People & process; both vertical & horizontal relationships
	Strategy	Successful program, well-managed system, profitable enterprise	Relational leadership with transformative process for God-horning changes & faithful/fruitful outcomes
	Evaluation	Worldly success & fame (mere horizontally)	Christ-like character individually and God-honoring growth institutionally

Figure 11-2. Popular Approaches vs. Relationally Transformational Discipleship at Two Levels

Another drawback to full-disclosure previews of teaching material is that it is not necessarily reproducible. The training that Jesus gave to the Twelve could be replicated in later generations with new technologies and new social relationships. Had Jesus been too detailed in his announcements ahead of time, it would have limited that reproducibility to the Jewish First Century context. Relational Discipleship in our day does well to take the same looser approach. We can and should point in general terms to the outcomes we want from the discipleship relationships. But giving too much detail about that relationship, or defining too narrowly the exact points of teaching, activities of spiritual life, or characteristics of spiritual relationships can actually work against the long-term accomplishment we want to achieve!

Appropriate Teaching Methods for Discipleship Outcomes

As a disciple-maker, Jesus is also our example in the way He taught people key lessons at the right moment. Educators talk about "learning readiness" and that is a powerful concept for discipleship too. When is a given person ready to receive a given lesson? At what stage of growth is a learner ready to grow into new knowledge, attitude, skill, relational health or spiritual life?

In the case of Jesus, we see Him sending the disciples first to the Lost Sheep of Israel, and later to the nations (Matthew 10:6 cf Matthew 28:18 - 20). The lessons learned in their familiar cultural environment taught them the principles of ministry. Later, in widely cross-cultural contexts, they applied those lessons across the diversity of national cultures.

Another example is the early talk about Jesus' suffering that was given in vague, imprecise terms. Later, He spoke clearly about the cross and the suffering that He and His disciples were called to (consider, for example, the detail included in the Upper Room Discourse John 13 - 17). He intentionally gave some lessons whose meaning would not be grasped until later (John 13: 7).

Appropriate Teaching Sequence for Discipleship Outcomes

As we consider relational discipleship, there is progression of topics that follow one another. While we could measure those in terms of time, it is more appropriate to say that one lesson begins after previous discipleship elements have been grasped. We begin with the basic truths, attitudes, affections, and activities of the Christian life. Later, we apply Christian truth to the realities of relational life: teaching and modeling faith, forgiveness, and perseverance that are hallmarks of Christian maturity. Growth continues, adding new lessons as circumstances require and as previous lessons are internalized. We prayerfully ask the Master Disciple-maker to guide us, as under shepherds, who also are touching the lives, hearts, hands and minds of a new generation of disciples.

James Plueddemann gives a powerful model for this progressive discipleship in his book, *Teaching Across Cultures*. Using a figure of speech that he has used in other works, he calls Christian educators (including disciple-makers) to have what he calls a "rail fence" and "a pilgrim" mentality.

The rail fence ties two apparently contradictory ideas together into one meaningful whole. Education, as one example of two apparently contradictory ideas that can co-exist, is both student-focused and content focused.

Another "rail fence" example is found in our concept of relational discipleship. Scripture calls us to build Biblical knowledge, spiritual disciplines, and human relationships all together. All are true and they are not self-contradictory. They are like the rails of a fence that are joined together by the vertical fence posts.[149]

The Pilgrim part of this model arises when we think of a pilgrim traveling across a wide landscape. In our technology age, we would make the trip with guidance by the GPS accessing computer and satellite information. But the pilgrims only knew they were heading west until they hit a given river, then

---

[149] James E. Plueddemann, *Teaching Across Cultures: Contextualizing Education for Global Mission* (Downers Grove, IL: IVP Academic, 2018), 19–23.

they would follow that north to the large hill, and so on. They knew the basic steps but their planning did not include detailed information for each step of the trip.

Relational discipleship knows where it is going, and knows what each of the disciple-makers along the way is intent on doing. In my case, I train global gospel workers toward better impact in a culture and language that is different than their own. I have a few concepts that I bring to the structured side of that discipleship, but I also tailor the process to the personality and life situation of the learner. I send them out to be involved in situations outside of their home culture, but I do not know the exact interactions that they will encounter. There are certain things that I ask the learners to experience. I specifically help to guide the training of these new intercultural workers, even though I am not present with them in all of their experiences. I know where we are heading, but there are many specific elements that I do not know. They learn as pilgrims; aware of the destination but having to set the course as they go.

There are stages in the formation of a mature disciple of Jesus Christ. The relational disciple-maker will keep that end in view, and at the same time will adjust and flex to focus on the right content and the right skill mix in the right horizontal, human relationships with the right vertical spiritual growth in view.

Outcomes of Relational Intercultural Discipleship

The outcomes that we expect from Relational Discipleship can be described as that individual progression of growth. We close this section by considering four outcomes that are at once distinct from one another, and yet also deeply related to one another: the outcomes of growth, maturity, change, and transformation.

Growth

By growth we mean adding new cognitive, emotional, and practical ability to what we already have developed. 2 Peter 3: 18 calls on believers to continue to grow "in the grace and the knowledge of the Lord Jesus Christ." We come into the Kingdom with some level of knowledge and some understanding of Jesus' character and the grace that He shows to us. But we continue to grow as well. We learn His patterns and His Word. We progress across time, learning more and more in both cognitive and experiential ways. One of the outcomes of discipleship is a disciple who is continually growing.

The following figure graphically depicts this kind of progressive transformation that illustrates the interactions of relationship with connection, interaction, and influence.

114

Relational Transformation

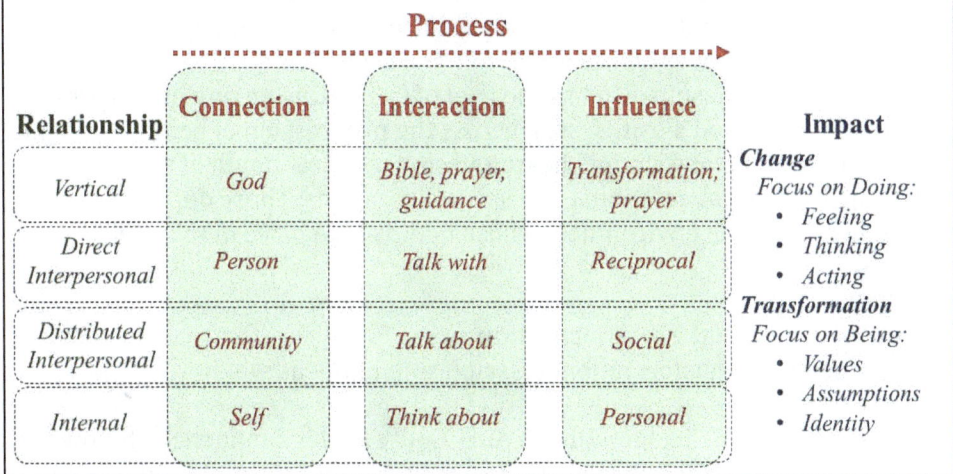

Process

Relationship	Connection	Interaction	Influence	Impact
Vertical	God	Bible, prayer, guidance	Transformation; prayer	**Change** *Focus on Doing:* • *Feeling*
Direct Interpersonal	Person	Talk with	Reciprocal	• *Thinking* • *Acting*
Distributed Interpersonal	Community	Talk about	Social	**Transformation** *Focus on Being:* • *Values*
Internal	Self	Think about	Personal	• *Assumptions* • *Identity*

Figure 11-3. Relational Transformation

Maturity

Discipleship wants to nurture that kind of growth. It wants to continue to see progress in spiritual, cognitive, emotional and behavioral terms until a person is living appropriate for his/her age and station in life. Maturity is not a single "mile-marker." Maturity is related to the situation in life and the cultural context. One can be "mature and complete, not lacking anything" (James 1:4), as a youth pastor at one time in their lives, and then later on grow again toward maturity as a Senior Pastor. Maturity has the implication of being well suited for a certain life situation. The young man can be mature for his age, and yet still need to grow further as he enters mid-life and older age.

Change

Change is defined as the shifting of activities according to variations in environment and in personal maturity. Transformation, on the other hand, is a shift in one's very being. Values, beliefs, understanding of life and one's place in life all undergo profound shifts in the process we call transformation. The most striking example of transformation is when one is "born again" (John 3). Obviously it is not a new physical birth, but the depth of transformation is so complete that one is for all intents, a new creature.

Transformation

The life transitions that we discussed in the previous chapter can be transformative. Moving from one culture to another can transform assumptions to the point that the old is forever gone, replaced with new understanding, new values, new perspectives on life.

Relational discipleship also has the goal of facilitating an ongoing process of transformation as God's truths, seen across the progression of being, belonging and becoming, open one's mind, heart and soul to a new depth of cognitive, emotional, behavioral, relational and spiritual realities. Those depths do not happen in a cognitive environment; those depths take place in relational discipleship.

Process of Relational Transformation

The process of transformational discipleship happens when:

Transformational Change= Divine Aid+ Godly leader's influence+ follower's positive response leading to transformation by entering faith community.[150]

The influence of a godly leader can include encouragement toward spiritual disciplines such as prayer, fasting, Bible memorization and Bible meditation. It can also be encouraged through service and sacrifice for the sake of the community. The figure below gives an example of Five-steps of Relational Convergence - five elements that foster growth and change. Through all of those elements (and others), the influence of a godly leader will itself be relational and will point toward deepening love relationship with God and with people. As that relational process continues, the expected outcome is growth and change in the disciple and in the community. And as Divine Aid also affects the disciple, a deep transformation produced by the power of the Spirit of God is what we prayerfully seek.

---

[150] Wan, "Relational Intercultural Leadership and Mentorship," 5.

116

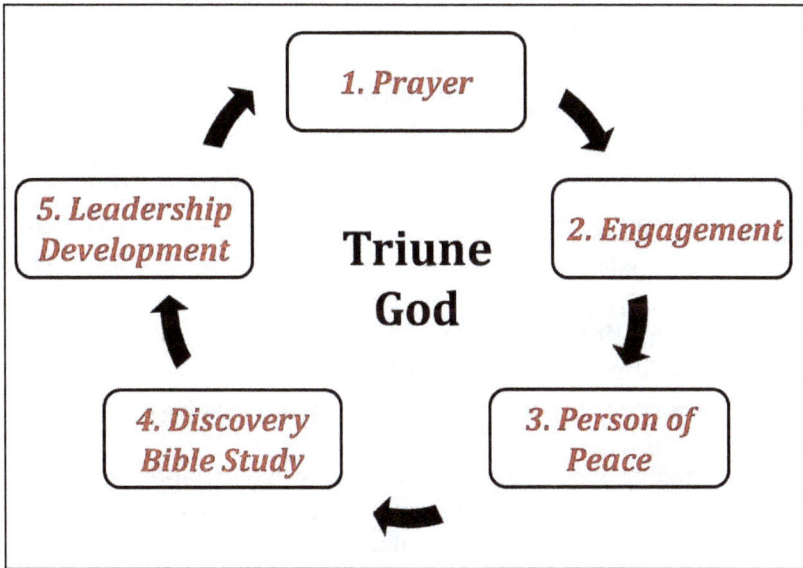

Figure 11-4. Five Steps of Relational Convergence

There is also a growing relational maturity from this 'becoming' element of discipleship. Within the faith community, God's Word calls people to transformational growth toward:

- Faithfulness in learning to minister with the gifts that the Spirit has given to each one for the building up of all (1 Cor. 12).
- Faithfulness in growing in Christian love to one another (1 Cor. 13).
- Faithfulness in passing on to others the spiritual and ministry lessons that each one has received (2 Tim. 2:2). This adds the element of both personal growth and the ability to teach others also.
- Faithfulness in pursuing growth in grace and knowledge (2 Peter 3:18).
- Faithfulness to "live a life worthy of the Lord and please him in every way: bearing fruit in every good work, growing in the knowledge of God, being strengthened with all power according to his glorious might so that you may have great endurance and patience, and giving joyful thanks to the Father." (Col. 1:10-12)

Summary and Conclusions

We can summarize the Becoming elements of relational discipleship by listing the outcomes that a relational disciple-maker wants to influence:

- Holistic growth in spiritual, cognitive, emotional, behavioral, and relational terms

- A clear picture of the outcomes of discipleship in the mind of the disciple-maker
- A general but not detailed description of outcomes to be shared with the disciple
- A progression of growth so that each step is followed in time by others. Growth is a step-by-step process
- Thinking in terms of fence-posts and pilgrims: allowing the process of growth to include goals and yet adjusting according to the realities of life and ministry. Apparently contradictory concepts and apparently contradictory applications begin to make sense in real life contexts; that is where relational discipleship takes place
- Recognizing the stages and processes we call growth, maturity, change, and transformation
- Being open to the depth of change that we call transformation as deeply held attitudes, beliefs and values are challenged by Christian discipleship. Transformation is the result of the Spirit of God opening hearts to the words taught by human disciple-makers (Acts 16:14).

Recall Figure 10-1:

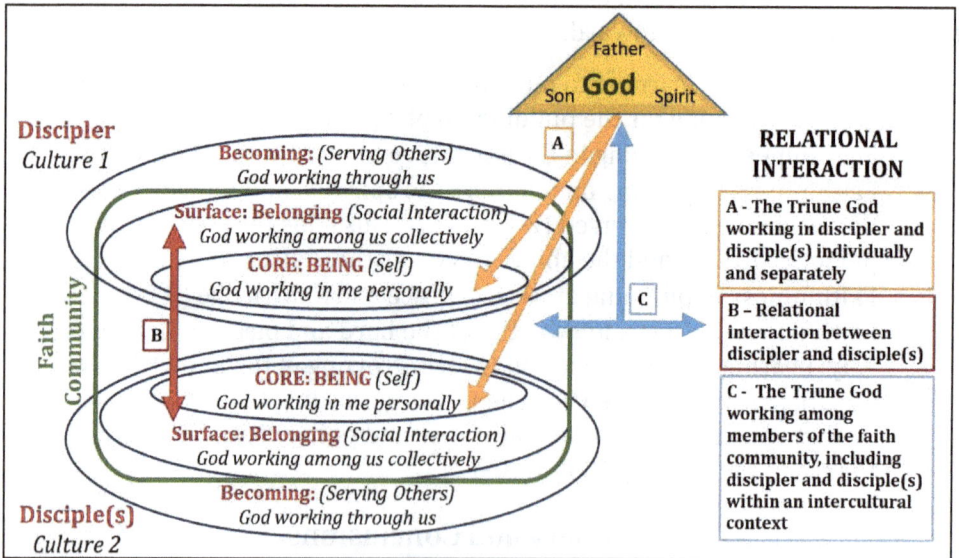

Figure 11-5. Intercultural Discipleship in Action

CHAPTER 12
Discipleship Summary

We conclude this review of relational discipleship and especially intercultural relational discipleship by summarizing this chapter around three questions:

- What is relational discipleship?
- Why do we recommend relational discipleship?
- How do we practice relational discipleship?

What is relational discipleship?

Relational discipleship, understood from the perspective of our study, is a deliberate process of relational teaching/learning aimed at growth toward Christian maturity. It is a form of discipleship that is

- Based on the characteristics of the disciple as a person and as a member of a culture.
- Developed within a relational community that includes church, culture, professional context, and emotional affinity.
- Leads to change, growth and transformation toward increasing godliness in personal characteristics of knowledge, feelings, skills, attitudes and relational health with both God and mankind.
- Leads to increasing ability to serve Christ as His servants on the earth.
- The result of God's Spirit interacting with the lessons taught by a godly human teacher/disciple-maker and accepted by a disciple who is open to learning and growing.

Why do we recommend relational discipleship and intercultural relational discipleship?

- Curriculum-based approaches to discipleship are mechanical, and as such are less realistic than the holistic growth that happens in full orbed human relationships
- Because most nations/cultures of the world are more relational than programmatic
- To make disciples in intercultural settings we need to use approaches that are understandable; this points to relational discipleship
- It models for us how to be "in the world" but not "of the world"

119

- It points to growth in all facets of life, in comparison to the curriculum-based approaches which focus on cognitive growth
- Relational discipleship is modeled over and over in Scripture, especially seen in the way that Jesus discipled the Twelve and in the way that Paul discipled Timothy and Titus.

How do we practice relational discipleship?

We practice relational discipleship:

- By being a deliberate learner of the personal and cultural characteristics of all of the Beings/beings and communities of believers that are involved
- By shaping discipleship activities according to expected and appropriate patterns of life and interaction in the life-contexts of the disciple
- By pursuing discipleship in community (*ecclesia*), in real life situations, and across the differences of culture
- By pursuing holistic, full-life growth and relationship
- Through flexible methods
- With discernment about the people and situations involved
- In prayerful and continuous deliberate vertical dependence on the Lord, knowing that He brings transformation
- With an openness to diversity of people within the relationships. Jesus worked with publicans and zealots
- Learner-centered as opposed to curriculum or teacher-centric
- Using the Bible's "one-another" relationships deliberately, and especially comforting and encouraging one another in times of persecution and hardship
- Through recognition and adaptation to how emotions are understood across cultures
- Through seeking wisdom to gauge the best amount of discipleship material to preview ahead of time
- By practicing "learning readiness" to judge when it is time to encourage another step of discipleship growth
- With a goal in mind. Making disciples is a team effort, and any one person has a particular part in the process. Knowing what areas are especially important for a growing Christian helps both the disciple maker and others who also will have a role in the future
- With clarity about the theoretical and practical meaning of growth, maturity, change and transformation within a given relationship

- Recognizing that we are called to teach as well as we possibly can, but it is in relationship with the Lord that transformation occurs

SECTION 4

TRANSFORMATIONAL GROWTH:

INTERCULTURAL MENTORSHIP

Various authors have found examples of mentoring relationships throughout the Bible. Jesus is a popular mentoring model, of course. Jeremy Peckham, for example, states, "The leadership of Jesus gives us a deeper insight into how we lead relationally. Jesus as the Son of God was able to command others to follow him, yet his approach to leading these followers was to build close relationships where he taught in small groups, challenged, mentored, and answered their questions."[151]

Other mentoring role models have been proposed from the Bible as well. Travis Snode suggests these mentoring relationships, with lessons from each: Jethro mentoring Moses, Moses mentoring Joshua, Moses mentoring Caleb, Samuel mentoring Saul, Jonathan mentoring David, Elijah mentoring Elisha,[152] Barnabas mentoring Paul; Barnabas mentoring John Mark; and Paul mentoring Timothy.[153] Walter Wright also suggests that Tychicus mentored Onesimus:

> When Paul sends Onesimus back to Colossae, he surely sends him out in the power of God. But he also sends with him a friend to support and encourage him as he returns home. Tychicus is there to encourage Onesimus as he faces Philemon: to confront Onesimus if fear makes him falter, to pave the way for

---

[151] Peckham, "Relational Leadership."

[152] Travis Snode, "Mentoring in the Old Testament (7 of 7) – Elijah and Elisha," *Into All The World* (blog), September 18, 2013, https://www.travissnode.com/articles/leadership/mentoring-old-testament-7-7-elijah-elisha/.

[153] Travis Snode, "Mentoring in the New Testament (5 of 5) – Paul and Timothy," *Into All The World* (blog), November 6, 2013, https://www.travissnode.com/articles/leadership/mentoring-new-testament-5-5-paul-timothy/.

him with Philemon and the Colossian church, and to pray for him and give advice as needed.[154]

We need to avoid reading our understanding of mentoring back into Scripture, but it can be helpful to consider and evaluate the lessons that have been proposed from the Bible and other sources. In this section, we will look at principles and examples of how mentoring can affect our being, belonging, and becoming, in the process of transformation.

.

---

[154] Wright, *Relational Leadership*, 42.

CHAPTER 13
Relational Intercultural Mentoring Introduction

As we have done with leadership and discipleship, in this section of the book we will look at the process of mentoring, and how it can help bring transformation to the people involved.

We have defined relational intercultural mentoring as *a reciprocal learning relationship in which the mentor and one or more mentees interact across cultural boundaries to influence each other to become more like Christ and better equipped to serve others*. This process is dependent on the commitment of each member to grow in their vertical relationship with the Triune God. Before we explore these steps of being, belonging, and becoming, however, we will unpack some of the elements involved in relational intercultural mentoring. We will being by exploring what mentoring is.

Mentoring

Fuller Seminary's leadership blogsite, *The Next Faithful Step*, includes this observation: "Mentoring is a broad term, and can cover guidance in handling challenges all the way from major questions of motivation and life goals down to day-to-day organizational logistics. Mentoring has also implied a range of personal patterns, from something close to imitation, to a relationship that prompts freedom and self-discovery."[155] Mentoring is closely related to leadership training and to discipleship. Walter Wright states,

> Mentoring is a strategy for leadership development, for personal leadership renewal. It fits within the larger context of relational leadership. Leadership is a relationship of influence that connects the character of the leader with the culture of the community and ultimately impacts the bottom line productivity of the organization. Mentors encourage leaders to reflect on who they are (pace), what is important (journey), and how they are shaping the culture of their organizations (relationships).[156]

---

[155] Theopulos, "Paul and Timothy," Fuller Seminary, *The Next Faithful Step* (blog), 2019, https://www.fuller.edu/next-faithful-step/resources/paul-and-timothy/.

[156] Walter C. Jr. Wright, *Mentoring: The Promise of Relational Leadership*, 2006 Reprint (Milton Keynes, Bucks, UK: Paternoster Press, 2004), xxix.

The figure below shows some of the relationships and growth that can happen in the lives of the mentee, the mentor, and the organization they are involved in.

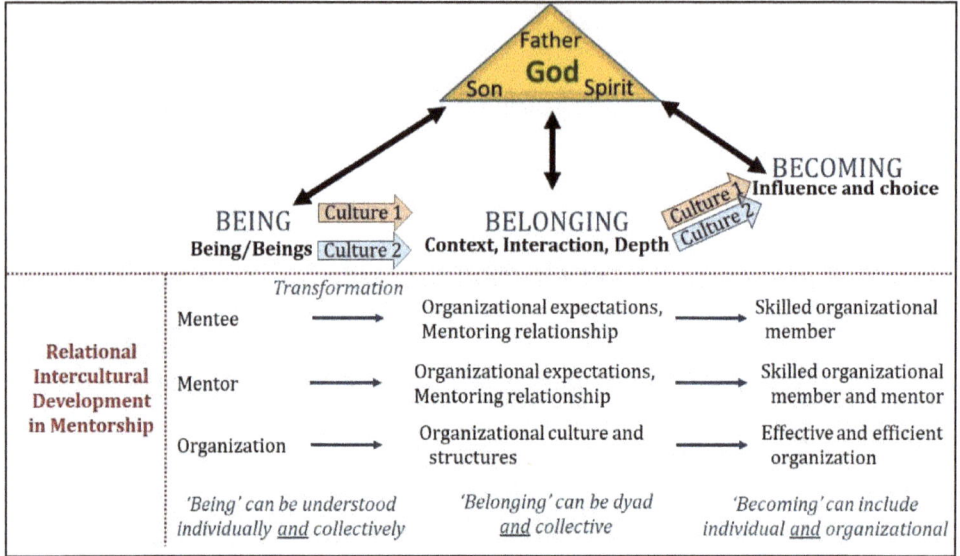

Figure 13-1. Transformational Development in Mentorship

Mentoring helps develop character and skills, so can be used as a means of both discipleship and leadership development, as well as in other aspects of growth. Since mentoring can take place in various contexts, and at various depths, a person can be involved in a number of mentoring relationships at the same time. We will explore some of the differences between formal and informal mentoring relationships in Chapter 15. A person might find that more than one formal mentoring relationship, each with separate structures and expectations, is difficult to maintain at the same time. But they could still benefit from having a number of informal mentoring connections, where spontaneous conversations result in encouragement and growth.

Relational Mentoring

Mentoring is a reciprocal relationship, in which mentors and mentees are all growing. This requires humble service on the part of the mentor, shown through a willingness to learn from those they are helping grow. This follows the example of Jesus' model of servant leadership (Luke 22:27; Mark 10:42-45). Lois Zachary notes that mentoring has become "a mutual discovery process in which both the mentor and mentee have something to bring to the relationship ("the give") and something to gain that broadens each of their perspectives ("the get"). Wisdom is not passed down but discovered and nurtured. This shift frees both partners to learn together."[157] We explore the implications of this collaborative process more when we discuss the 'belonging' aspects of mentoring in chapter 15.

Mentors and mentees need to have a connection that allows them to trust each other and interact honestly. Their interactions are deliberately influential, designed to help the mentee in their transformational growth. Matt Thomas contrasts mentoring to the relationship between managers and staff:

> As a mentor, the relationship with a protégé is characterized by depth and personal commitment, focusing on broader objectives and encouraging mentees to ask relevant questions and think in new and creative ways. Alternatively, managers mange for profitability, productivity, and business outcomes. The depth and personal commitment Jesus made to his disciples was an influential trait that shaped these men as future leaders and continued to model the pattern of leadership by intentionally creating-through deep, committed relationships – other Christian leaders.[158]

Stephen and Mary Lowe describe social networks as "the connections people have with each other, the interactions that transpire across the connections, and the influence that results from these connective interactions."[159] Relational mentoring is one form that these connections and interactions can take, for the purpose of achieving specific types of growth.

Relational Intercultural Mentoring

Let us now add a third element: what might relational mentoring look like when it crosses cultural boundaries? Bramwell Osula and Steve Irvin define an intercultural mentoring relationship as one "when mentor and mentee are from different cultures. Both mentor and mentee bring to the relationship values and assumptions that are culturally based. By understanding the influence of culture on attitudes, expectations, and behaviors, leaders may increase their cultural awareness and improve intercultural mentoring practices."[160] They argue:

---

[157] Lois J. Zachary, *The Mentor's Guide: Facilitating Effective Learning Relationships*, Second (San Francisco: Jossey-Bass, 2012), 3.

[158] Thomas, *The Indispensable Mark of Christian Leadership,* 110.

[159] Lowe and Lowe, *Ecologies of Faith in a Digital Age*, 124.

[160] Bramwell Osula and Steve M. Irvin, "Cultural Awareness in Intercultural Mentoring: A Model for Enhancing Mentoring Relationships," *International Journal of Leadership Studies, School of Global Leadership & Entrepreneurship, Regent University* 5, no. 1 (2009): 38.

The model of cultural awareness forces the leader to adopt the posture of a student of cultures, both of his or her own culture as well as of the culture of the mentee. Organizations with existing mentoring strategies of leadership development in intercultural contexts can enhance those strategies by introducing potential mentors and mentees to this cultural awareness model, contributing to the enhancement of intercultural mentoring relationships.[161]

Mentors should be aware of their own culture and that of their mentees, and make adjustments to the mentoring structure and interactions in order to help the mentee grow as much as possible. In some cultures, for example, mentees may be more comfortable and open to insights in a group setting. Mentoring models in North America and Europe might focus on one-on-one interaction, but group mentoring may be more effective in cultures that focus more on collective interaction and benefit than on individuals.

The third-culture model that Osula and Irvin propose is illustrated by Figure 13-2. They suggest that general cultural awareness, cultural self-awareness, and situation-specific awareness contribute to the development of a third-culture perspective, which results in culturally appropriate behavior and meaningful relationships.[162] They define this third-culture perspective as a "new composite which, while developed from the individual perspectives of each cultural actor, nevertheless transcends these localized or specific perspectives, presenting an alternate, or *third-view*, culture."[163]

---

[161] Osula and Irvin, *Cultural Awareness in Intercultural Mentoring*, 46.
[162] Osula and Irvin, *Cultural Awareness in Intercultural Mentoring*, 45.
[163] Osula and Irvin, *Cultural Awareness in Intercultural Mentoring*, 44.

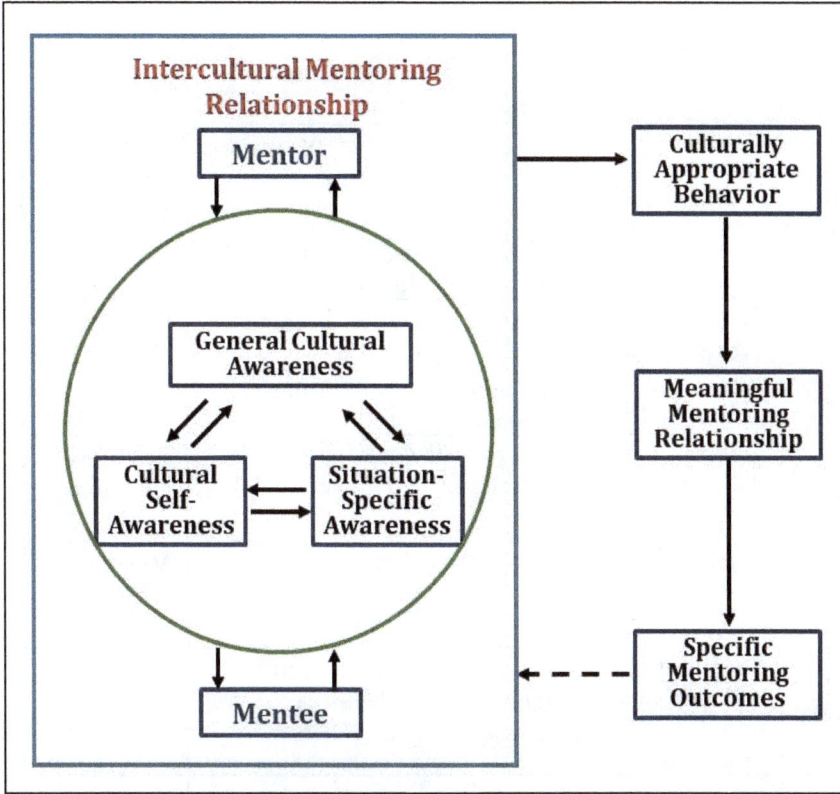

Figure 13-2. Conceptual model of the relationship between cultural awareness and intercultural mentoring relationships.[164]

Osula and Irvin also provide a chart listing elements and theories of cultural awareness by various authors, as shown in the figure below. These references list some of the key elements of intercultural mentoring, including cultural sensitivity, empathy, mindfulness, and competence.

---

[164] Osula and Irvin, *Cultural Awareness in Intercultural Mentoring*, 46.

Term	Key Principle	Description	Author
Cultural Sensitivity	"Difference"	6 stages from ethnocentrism to ethnorelativism	Bennett, 1986
	"Sensitivity"	(a) interest in other cultures; (b) notice of cultural differences; (c) modify behavior as mark of respect for other cultures	Bhawuk & Brislin, 1992
	Perpetual Schema	(a) accurate cultural schema (b) ideographic data	Ridley et al., 1994
Cultural Empathy	Frame of reference	Temporary shift in a frame of reference	Bennett, 1986
	Cultural differences	Change behavior when interacting with others	Brislin & Yoshida, 1994
	Communicating Understanding	Sensitivity and empathy	Mullavey-O'Byrne, 1997
Mindfulness	Readiness to shift one's frame of readiness	(a) Mindlessness (reactive stage) (b) Mindfulness (proactive stage)	Ting-Toomey, 1999
Cultural Competence	Appropriate conduct	Mutually competent behavior	Collier, 1989
	"Intercultural communication competence"	Intercultural Behavioral Assessment Indices	Ruben, 1976
	"Functional awareness"	Management of behavior in intercultural contexts	Hoopes, 1981

Figure 13-3. Aspects of Cultural Awareness[165]

A key element in these various perspectives to intercultural mentoring is a deliberate awareness of the people involved in the relationship, and a willingness to invest the time and effort necessary to understand and benefit each other.

We have introduced the mentoring, relational, and intercultural elements of relational intercultural mentoring. In the following chapters, we will explore

---

[165] Osula and Irvin, *Cultural Awareness in Intercultural Mentoring*, 42.

how the 'being,' 'belonging,' and 'becoming' of mentors and mentees can reflect and enhance intentional transformational growth.

CHAPTER 14
Being in Intercultural Mentoring

In this chapter, we will focus on the people involved in a transformational mentoring relationship. We will explore some of the experiences, needs, and strengths they bring to mentoring. These all affect the ways a mentor might build the relationship to intentionally leverage these elements for transformation.

Beings/beings

The people involved in a mentoring relationship shape the interactions and consequences of the relationship. This includes the Persons of the Trinity, when the mentor and mentees are growing in their vertical relationships with God. James Plueddemann states, "Three things that shape us are:
- our common human nature,
- the culture that fashioned us, and
- individual personalities that make us unique."[166]

We will explore some of the cultural and personal aspects that people bring to a mentoring relationship that impact the connections, interactions, and influence within that relationship.

Cultural Aspects of Being

We will take a deeper look how an intercultural context can affect ongoing mentoring interactions when we look at the process of 'belonging' in Chapter 15. For now we will focus on the impact that culture has on each individual at a 'being' level.

Various authors have proposed lists of cultural traits and values that affect intercultural interactions.[167]In exploring the difficulties involved in cross-cultural ministry, James Plueddemann examines four examples of cultural values, which are described in the Figure 14-1.

---

[166] Plueddemann, *Leading Across Cultures*, 72. Formatting changed for emphasis.

[167] See for example, David Livermore, *Leading with Cultural Intelligence: The Real Secret to Success*, 2nd ed. (New York: Amacom, 2015), Erin Meyer, *The Culture Map: Breaking through the Invisible Boundaries of Global Business* (New York: PublicAffairs, 2018), and Geert Hofstede, Gert Jan Hofstede, and Michael Minkov, *Cultures and Organizations: Software of the Mind: Intercultural Cooperation and Its Importance for Survival*, 3rd ed. (New York: McGraw-Hill, 2010).

Cultural Value	Description
Context	The degree of sensitivity to what is happening around people: in a high-context culture, people pay attention to the concrete world around them. Low-context culture focus on explicit communication and ideas
Power	High-power-distance cultures assume that the leader has more authority, respect and status symbols, can make unilateral decisions, and be obeyed without question. Leaders in low-power-distance cultures prefer a consultative, participative or democratic decision-making style
Individualism	In an individualistic culture, the community exists to meet the needs of individuals; accomplishing a task is more important than relationships. In a collective culture, individuals seek to foster the good of the group; building relationships is the means for accomplishing a task.
Ambiguity	Cultures with a low tolerance for ambiguity (high uncertainty avoidance) minimize insecurity by having policies, timetables and detailed planning. Cultures with a high tolerance for ambiguity (low uncertainty avoidance) live more in the present.

Figure 14-1. Examples of Cultural Values[168]

Cultural traits have both positive or negative influences on the people within that culture, and those that they are in contact with. In this book, we have used the terms trangressional decline and transformational growth to descibe these influences on individuals. Edmund Chan suggests four cultural influences today that need to be addressed in discipling and mentoring relationships.

Culture	Description
Selfish	lacks identity found only in the love of God
Pragmatic	places little value on truth
Consumer	places personal rights above respect for authority and compassion for the needs of others
Workaholic	prioritizes activism over rest, peace, and renewal of spirit

Figure 14-2. Chan's List of Cultural Influences[169]

---

[168] James E. Plueddemann, *Leading Across Cultures: Effective Ministry and Mission in the Global Church* (Downers Grove, IL: IVP Academic, 2009), 78, 95, 113, 120. 129.

[169] Adapted from Edmund Chan, *Mentoring Paradigms: Reflections on Mentoring, Leadership, and Discipleship* (Oklahoma City: Lifestyle Impact Publishing, 2008), 122–23.

Let us explore one of these influences in a bit more detail, as an example of the impact it can have on mentoring. Andy Johnson attributes the pragmatic nature that exists in the Western Church of valuing results over the faithful obedience to the Word of God. He coins the term 'Evangelical Pragmatism' which he describes as the West's "willingness to overlook or even contradict what the Bible says, for the sake of what appears to work visibly and immediately."[170] Johnson warns that if our functional authority is man-centered and concentrated on results, the church could be led astray. [171] The symptoms of this shift include basing decisions on results rather than careful exegesis and understanding of the Bible, evaluating ministry by numbers instead of faithfulness to Christ.

Personal Aspects of Being

Identity and roles

The ways in which people view themselves and their roles within the mentoring relationship impact the closeness of the mentoring connection, the conversations that take place within those connections, and the resulting influence that mentors and mentees have on each other.

Timothy Curran and his fellow researchers propose a "Relationship Quality" variable that affects the effectiveness of mentoring. They hypothesize that Relationship Quality is related to (1) the personality of the mentee; (2) the personality of the mentor; and (3) the interaction of the personalities of mentees and mentors.[172] Each person is an individual. We are all shaped by common experiences of being human, and by various cultural influences that we have experienced. We also are impacted by the family settings we were raised in, and the groups that we belong to. In addition, we are shaped by our personal temperaments, strengths, weaknesses, experiences, and goals. These all impact our relationships and interactions, including our relationships as mentors and mentees.

Carson Pue argues, "Abiding, staying attached, recognizing who is at the core of who you are and revolving your leadership around this core- that is what mature leaders do."[173] He contrasts the effects of seeing ourselves as children of

---

[170] Andy Johnson, "Pragmatism, Pragmatism Everywhere!" *9Marks* (blog), February 2, 2010, https://www.9marks.org/article/pragmatism-pragmatism-everywhere/.

[171] Johnson, *Pragmatism, Pragmatism Everywhere!*

[172] Timothy Curran et al., "The Effect of Personality on Mentoring," *The Chronicle of Mentoring & Coaching* 1, no. Special Issue 10 (December 2017): 384.

[173] Carson Pue, *Mentoring Leaders: Wisdom for Developing Character, Calling, and Competency* (Grand Rapids: Baker Books, 2005), 53.

God, and seeing ourselves as orphans. The differences are summarized in Figure 14-3. He states,

> Self-awareness is at the very core of your development as a leader. You must have an accurate self-awareness, not simply of your abilities, gifts, and skills but also of the shadow side of your life as a leader. Most importantly, leaders must have absolute clarity on who they are as children of God. Self-awareness is about finding and being secure in your identity in Christ.[174]

---

[174] Pue, *Mentoring Leaders* , 21.

Identity Comparison	Orphaned from God	Child of God
Condition	Bondage	Liberty
Dependency	Independent/self-reliant	Interdependent/ Acknowledges need
Expression of Love	Guarded and conditional; based upon others' performance as you seek to get your own needs met	Open, patient, and affectionate as you lay your life and agendas down in order to meet the needs of others
Future	Fight for what you can get	Releases your inheritance
Handling Others' Faults	Accusation and exposure in order to make yourself look good by making others look bad	Love covers as you seek to restore others in a spirit of love and gentleness
Image of God	See God as Master	See God as a loving Father
Motive behind Disciplines	Duty, earning God's favor or no motivation at all	Pleasure and delight
Motive for Service	A need for personal achievement as you seek to impress God and others, or no motivation to serve at all	Service that is motivated by a deep gratitude for being unconditionally loved and accepted by God
Peer Relationships	Competition, rivalry, and jealousy toward others' success and position	Humility and unity as you value others and are able to rejoice in their blessings and success

Figure 14-3. Functioning from Your Core as a Child of God[175]

Lois Zachary explains that the 'flow' of a mentor's facilitation "will always depend on the needs of the mentee. Some learners may need more support and direction to feel comfortable with the process, while others feel prepared and are ready to go to work immediately."[176] She lists ways in which mentoring has

---

[175] Adapted from Pue, *Mentoring Leaders,* 53–54. These are a selection from his full list.
[176] Zachary, *Mentor's Guide,* 48

changed over the past decades. A number of these changes are related to the ways in which mentors and mentees see themselves and their roles within the relationship. Her list is given in Figure 14.4.

Mentoring Element	Changing Paradigm	Adult Learning Principle
Mentee role	From: Passive receiver To: Active partner	Adults learn best when they are involved in diagnosing, planning, implementing, and evaluating their own learning.
Mentor role	From: Authority To: Facilitator	The role of the facilitator is to create and maintain a supportive climate that promotes the conditions necessary for learning to take place.
Learning process	From: Mentor directed and responsible for the mentee's learning To: Self-directed with the mentee responsible for own learning	Adult learners have a need to be self-directing.
Length of relationship	From: Calendar focus To: Goal determined	Readiness for learning increases when there is a specific need to know.
Mentoring relationship	From: One life = one mentor; one mentor = one mentee To: Multiple mentors over a lifetime and multiple modalities for mentoring; individual, group, and peer models	Life's reservoir of experience is a primary learning resource; the life experiences of others enrich the learning process.
Setting	From: Face-to-face To: Multiple and varied venues and opportunities	Adult learners have an inherent need for immediacy of application.
Focus	From: Product oriented: knowledge transfer and acquisition To: Process oriented: Critical reflection and application	Adults respond best to learning when they are internally motivated to learn.

Figure 14-4. Elements in the Learner-Centered Mentoring Paradigm[177]

---

[177] Zachary, The Mentor's Guide, 6.

Goals

The structure and results of mentoring are impacted by the identities and roles that mentors and mentees bring to their relationship; they are also affected by the goals that the members bring. In Chapter 17, we will explore in more depth some of the influences that mentoring can have on the lives of both mentors and mentees; here, we will focus on some of the intentions that each member might have going into the relationship.

Chan states, "Character is everything. A person's wholeness and basic commitment to integrity are paramount in ministry. These reveal the inner moral compass and ensure the honor of God and the Church."[178] Randy Reese and Robert Loane agree on the importance of character, and add two other areas of formation that are important to address in mentoring. These are listed in the following figure, along with key questions for each area.

Type	Focus	Key question
Character formation	Relates to our spiritual maturation, which is concerned with the ongoing dynamics and qualities of our inner life or heart	How are we giving attention to the shaping of the person?
Skill formation	Concerned with the skills, knowledge and practice related to the work of leadership	What is involved in the work of leadership?
Strategic formation	Looks at the development of a coherent ministry philosophy of values, which serves to steer the person toward a more effective, focused and purposeful life and ministry	How do I deepen my own inner life, while at the same time investing in the formation of others?

Figure 14-5. Three critical formations[179]

Walter Wright states,

Mentoring is a relationship with a purpose. There is no formula, no ideal model, and no program of steps to success. It is a relationship connected by a shared interest in learning and growth, and it must be constantly nurtured and recreated. It has purpose and structure defined by the learning needs of the mentoree and shaped by the wisdom and experience of the mentor.[180]

---

[178] Chan, *Mentoring Paradigms*, 100–101.

[179] Randy D. Reese and Robert Loane, *Deep Mentoring: Guiding Others on Their Leadership Journey* (Downers Grove, IL: Inter-Varsity Press, 2012), 64–65. Adapted into table format.

[180] Wright, *Relational Leadership*, 68.

Lois Zachary also describes the intentionality of the mentoring relationship: "As a mentor, you need to be skilled at facilitating adult learning--engaging mentees as active participants in their own learning by encouraging self-reflection and self-authorship. In essence, you are creating conditions that enable mentees to learn."[181]

Summary

In intercultural mentoring, the mentor is helping the mentees prepare to live and minister to people that have different cultural assumptions, values, and behaviors than the mentor. Therefore, the mentor must be careful to not impose goals or solutions that make it harder for the mentees to relate to and minister to the people they are serving. Mentoring is a person-centered process: it focuses on the Person of God, and the impact that God desires to have in the lives of mentors, mentees, and those people that they minister to.

---

[181] Zachary, *Mentor's Guide*, 47

CHAPTER 15
Belonging in Intercultural Mentoring

In this chapter, we will focus on the benefits that can occur when mentors and mentees make an effort to develop a sense of deep connection and belonging. Randy Reese and Robert Loane note the problems that arise when leadership training takes place without an emphasis on relationships: "So much of what passes for leadership development today lacks interpersonal investment, life upon life."[182] They use the illustration of a guide to describe the mentor's role in the development of leaders in Christian ministry. "Simply telling others where they must go won't cut it. The journey must be shared."[183] The authors use the example of Jesus and his disciples to highlight the importance of relationship in this mentoring journey: "The life of Jesus must be seen and held as the unique model worthy of imitation for Christians. For in Jesus we discover not only a model for the journey but an invitation to this life together."[184]

How do we build these connections between the mentor and mentees, and how do we intentionally interact within those connections so we achieve meaningful influence? We will explore how context, interaction, and depth help develop the 'belonging' where these connections and interactions can take place.

Context

The contexts of mentoring interactions shape the goals and structure of the conversations. Jack Mezirow states, "The justification for much of what we know and believe, our values, and our feelings depends on the context...in which they are embedded."[185] Zachary lists some of the elements of these contexts: "All mentoring relationships are grounded in context: the circumstances, conditions, and contributing forces that affect how we connect, interact with, and learn from one another."[186]

---

[182] Reese, Randy D. and Robert Loane, *Deep Mentoring: Guiding Others on Their Leadership Journey* (Downer's Grove, IL: IV Press, 2012), 23.

[183] Reese and Loane, *Deep Mentoring*, 23.

[184] Reese and Loane, *Deep Mentoring*, 179.

[185] Jack Mezirow, *Learning as Transformation: Critical Perspectives on a Theory in Progress*, 1st ed, The Jossey-Bass Higher and Adult Education Series (San Francisco: Jossey-Bass, 2000), 3.

[186] Zachary, *The Mentor's Guide*, 34.

She also notes the challenges that can arise because of overlapping contexts. "Context plays a critical role, yet it is an elusive and difficult concept to grasp because our contexts are multilayered: we never operate in just one context."[187] We will look at some of the challenges and opportunities that can arise from cultural, corporate, and environmental settings.

Cultural Contexts

In Chapter 14, we looked at cultural values that can shape an individual. Here, we will take a brief look at how mentors can be deliberate and careful to communicate and well in an intercultural relationship. Ralph Winter writes about the dangers of expecting unity in the church to include uniformity to our cultural traditions. He states, "In our weak moments we may all have hoped for, or anticipated, a global church of Jesus Christ that would all speak English and reflect exactly the flavor and customs of the cultural tradition in which we ourselves have been reared."[188] Winter goes on to say that would be a tragedy of uniformity. "We are much richer due to our differences, different emphases, different perspectives. It may not be obvious but it really does take a multi-cultural movement to understand a multicultural Bible. Our unity across the globe is not the same as uniformity." This desire for cultural uniformity can take place within mentoring relationships also, but we lose the opportunity to see more of God and his design as we take time to understand the perspective of mentees and mentors from other cultures.

Zachary gives an inventory of "cross-cultural mentoring skills" to help mentors intentionally interact across cultural boundaries:

- Reflective listening: using the skills of attending, clarifying, and confirming
- Checking for understanding
- Maintaining cultural self-awareness
- Providing and receiving feedback
- Maintaining global perspective
- Reading between the lines (keying into feelings)
- Suspending judgment
- Maintaining emotional versatility
- Exercising cultural flexibility
- Creating culturally appropriate networking opportunities

---

187 Zachary, *The Mentor's Guide*, 34.

188 Winter, Ralph, "A Missiological Approach to the Non-Christian Religions." In Christian Witness in Pluralistic Contexts in the Twenty-First Century, Edited by Enoch Wan, EMS Series No: 11. Pasadena: William Carey Library, 2004, 21.

- Modifying communication style to accommodate cultural differences
- Sensitivity to varying cultural perceptions of time, space, authority, and protocol.[189]

An example will illustrate ways in which mentors might adapt their approaches in an intercultural mentoring situation. In North American culture, privacy is highly valued, making the biblical principle of brotherly love and community a challenge. But there is value of working together in teams. In a training team, the members should represent diverse backgrounds and life situations so that any given trainee can see cross-cultural ministry modeled by people who come from backgrounds similar to his or hers.[190] In a mentoring relationship, this might take the form of spending more time with one another, sharing a meal together, allowing time for conversing with one another, and doing things together in "community locations."[191]

Personal and Corporate Contexts

Reese and Loane state, "...we begin to listen to the particular situation and place. This discipline of deep and reverent listening must be brought to each of our unique contexts.[192] Mentoring from a relational paradigm recognizes God's authority as revealed in His word to speak into every aspect of both the mentor's and mentee's lives. The authority of Scripture (2 Peter 1:3, 4, 20; 2 Tim. 3:16, 17) must be recognized by both parties.

The setting of mentoring can be formal or informal. Zachary describes the difference as follows:

Formal mentoring is commonly associated with words like *organized*, *proscribed*, *structured*, *facilitated*, and *supported*. But the term itself actually refers to mentoring that is conducted under the umbrella of an organizational entity, such as a business or a school. Program parameters are defined for the mentoring partnership and include both structural and accountability mechanisms. Programmatic and relationship expectations, requirements for eligibility, and program goals and outcomes give this mentoring formality.

---

[189] Zachary, *The Mentor's Guide*, 47.

[190] Enoch Wan and Mark Hedinger, *Relational Missionary Training* (Skyforest, Urban Loft Publishers, 2017), 200.

[191] W. Jay Moon, *Intercultural Discipleship: Learning from Global Approaches to Spiritual Formation* (Grand Rapids: Baker Academic, 2017), 218.

[192] Reese and Loane, *Deep Mentoring*, 209.

Informal mentoring relationships are usually described as unstructured, casual, need based, and natural…Informal mentoring relationships can run the gamut from casual conversations or situational and information sharing to structured and formalized relationships. Each relationship proceeds at its own pace and on its own timetable.

Even in formal mentoring, each relationship structure varies depending on the learning needs and style of the mentoring partners. Once you are inside and working the relationship, it becomes a dance of two or more people coming together in partnership to move learning and development forward.[193]

Whether the mentoring is a formal arrangement established within an organization, or an informal set of conversations, the context impacts the ways in which the members interact.

Environmental Contexts

The environment of mentoring conversations also impacts the relationship and outcomes. It is helpful to recognize these environmental contexts and evaluate how the interactions can best be conducted within them, to meet the mentoring goals.

For example, the mentoring relationship may take place over a distance, by the means of technology. Stephen and Mary Lowe remind us that the work of the Holy Spirit is not limited by the proximity of the people being transformed: "Our study of the ecology of spiritual formation has led us to recognize that God's Spirit can perform his miraculous work of transformation when Christians are gathered and when they are scattered."[194] In a mentoring relationship facilitated by phone or computer, the Holy Spirit can still work to produce spiritual growth in both the mentee and the mentor.

Interaction

How do the mentor and mentees engage with each other, in order to meet their goals? Walter Wright states, "Research has shown that, while knowledge can be transmitted in a variety of forms and media, learning occurs in interactive relationships. Mentoring is an interactive learning relationship, providing a significant point of connection in an increasingly fragmented

---

[193] Zachary, *The Mentor's Guide*, 68.
[194] Lowe and Lowe, *Ecologies of Faith in a Digital Age*, 200.

world."[195] Likewise, Randy Reese and Robert Loane describe the purposes of these mentoring interactions:

> Essentially, spiritual mentoring is a relationship between two or more people and the Holy Spirit, where the people can discover, through the already present action of God, three things: (1) intimacy with God (who is God?), (2) identity as beloved children of God (Who am I?), and (3) a unique voice for kingdom responsibility (What am I to do with my life?)[196]

These questions highlight a believer's vertical relationship with God, and the impact that 'becoming' should have on our identity and our actions. But as we examine transformational growth, we should also be deliberate in considering the horizontal relationships, both inside and outside of mentoring, that influence this growth. Perhaps changing the second question to "Who are we?" helps us reflect more deeply on the connections that the beloved children of God have with each other. This would also allow us to consider the influence that we can have on each other as we each consider our own 'voice' and actions, and how they can help further God's kingdom.

Interaction can take a variety of forms within mentoring. Zachary states that mentors "can facilitate learning in many ways, all the while listening, empowering, coaching, challenging, teaching, collaborating, aiding, assisting, supporting, expediting, easing, simplifying, advancing, and encouraging." [197]

Mentors are people who listen and speak deliberately, in order to help the mentee in the process of transformational growth. As we look at this intentional interaction, we will briefly explore Ephesians 4:29. In this verse, Paul commands us to, "let no corrupting talk come out of your mouths, but only such as is good for building up, as fits the occasion, that it may give grace to those who hear" (ESV). This verse contrasts things that should not be said, and things that should. Jamieson, Fausset, and Brown state that *sapros* meant "insipid," without "the salt of grace" (Colossians 4:6), so came to mean "worthless," then "corrupt."[198] John Stott says that the word was used of rotten trees and rotten fruit, then explains:

> When applied to rotten talk, whether this is dishonest, unkind or vulgar, we may be sure that in some way it hurts the hearers. Instead, we are to use our unique gift of speech constructively, for edifying, that is to build people up

---

[195] Wright, *Relational Leadership*, 66.

[196] Reese and Loane, *Deep Mentoring*, 189.

[197] Zachary, *Mentor's Guide*, 48

[198] Robert Jamieson, A. R. Fausset, and David Brown, *Commentary Practical and Explanatory on the Whole Bible.*, 2nd Printing (Oak Harbor, WA: Zondervan Publishing House, 1962), 352.

and not damage or destroy them, as fits the occasion. Then our words will impart grace to those who hear.[199]

Francis Foulkes states, "The test of conversation is not just 'Am I keeping my words true and pure?' but 'Are my words being used to *impart grace to those who hear?*' The *grace* of the Lord's own words, the love and blessing which they conveyed, is spoken of in Luke 4:22. The utterance of the Christian is to be characterized by the same *grace* (cf. Col. 3:16; 4:6)."[200] Jerome wrote, "Whenever we say what is not in season or inappropriate for the context, or that which does not contribute to the good of the hearers...even if we do no direct harm, yet we are not thereby building up."[201]

In a mentoring relationship, we should be intentional about the words that are spoken. As mentors, we need to avoid unfruitful and unproductive words, and focus on conversations that:

- Build up and edify the mentees. Is the conversation helping them be more aware of God, themselves, and the people around them, and helping them better reflect God's character and love?
- Are appropriate to the specific occasion. Are we aware of the needs of our mentees, and focused on the contexts surrounding the interaction?
- Give grace to those we are speaking to. As a result of this interaction, are the mentees more aware of God's grace in their lives, and more intentional about being conduits of grace to those they are in contact with?

Mentoring interactions, whether in a formal or informal context, can meet these criteria, but it requires being intentional about our words, and being dependent on the Holy Spirit to guide these conversations.

There are various models that shape our mentoring conversations. In describing online education, John Cartwright and his coauthors describe various approaches, and call for a higher level of expectation:

Considering the need for Spiritual formation within the lives of the students, the role of the online faculty member should be more than a "sage on the stage," or even "a guide on the side." By sage on the stage, it is meant that the faculty member is seen as just a conveyor of information. By guide on the

[199] John Stott, *The Message of Ephesians: God's New Society*, Revised edition, The Bible Speaks Today (IVP, 2020), 189.

[200] Francis Foulkes, *The Letter of Paul to the Ephesians: An Introduction and Commentary*, 2nd edition (Leicester, England : Grand Rapids, MI: Eerdmans Pub Co, 1989), 138–46.

[201] Jerome, *Epistle to the Ephesians*, 2.4.29, in Mark J. Edwards, *Galatians, Ephesians, Philippians*, 179.

side the faculty member is seen as someone who comes alongside the students and walks them through the learning process (guidance/mentorship). Information transfer and guidance are both important elements to the educational process; however, for online ministerial training, they are not enough. Information transfer or mentorship without the goal of formation falls short of the goal of ministerial training. The role of the faculty member concerns more than the transferring of information; the role of the faculty member is a formative role within the life of the student. Consequently, the faculty member's role becomes "a model to follow".[202]

The options that Cartwright lists do not need to be mutually exclusive. In mentoring, as in teaching, there are times where it is appropriate to give content, and times to guide by encouraging thoughtful interaction. In all of those interactions, however, the mentor (and teacher) should be a model of Christian maturity and Christ-likeness.

Edmund Chan lists values, steps, and competencies that can help produce beneficial mentoring interactions. These are listed in the chart below.

Element	Description
Values	• Grace • Growth • Godliness
Steps	• Discovering the truth • Applying the truth • Reaping the benefits • Passing on the truth
Competencies	• Know the mentee (shepherding role includes caring, counseling, coaching) • Display teachability: ask the right questions, understand the mentee's learning type and preference • Be a God-centered leader who leads by example and vision from God

Figure 15-1. Chan's Key Elements of Mentoring[203]

It is important to remember that mentees have choices. They can choose whether to interact with the mentor, and whether to implement any action steps they agree to in the conversations. Mentors need to be especially careful

---

[202] John Cartwright et al., *Teaching the World: Foundations for Online Theological Education* (Nashville: B&H Academic, 2017), 100.
[203] Chan, *Mentoring Paradigms*, 50–64.

of how to encourage mentees in intercultural contexts. One approach that can be helpful in some settings is 'Nudge theory.' It uses small interventions, in the form of indirect suggestions and positive reinforcement, to influence an individual's decisions and actions. Richard Thaler and Cass Sunstein define a nudge as "any aspect of the choice architecture that alters people's behavior in a predictable way without forbidding any options or significantly changing their economic incentives. To count as a mere nudge, the intervention must be easy and cheap to avoid."[204] Educational researchers are finding that these small interventions that encourage positive behavior are making a difference in students' performance.[205]

Accountability is a key piece of mentoring interactions. Pue writes, "Accountability is one way to lessen the areas of vulnerability in our lives as leaders, and every leader should be expected to practice both external and internal accountability."[206] Scripture also speak to the need for accountability:

- "Wounds from a friend can be trusted" (Proverbs 27:6)
- "The pleasantness of one's friend springs from his earnest counsel" (Proverbs 27:10)
- "Therefore confess your sins to one another and pray for one another, that you may be healed. The prayer of a righteous person has great power as it is working" (James 5:16).

Rosario Calderon implemented and evaluated a mentoring program for marketplace ministry that focuses on relational spiritual mentorship. She noted that both vertical and horizontal interaction is needed throughout the mentoring process. This is displayed in Figure 15.2.

---

[204] Richard H. Thaler and Cass R. Sunstein, *Nudge: Improving Decisions about Health, Wealth, and Happiness* (London: Yale University Press, 2008), 6.

[205] Flower Darby and James M. Lang, *Small Teaching Online: Applying Learning Science in Online Classes*, first edition (San Francisco, CA: Jossey-Bass, 2019). Electronic location 2827.

[206] Pue, *Mentoring Leaders*, 254

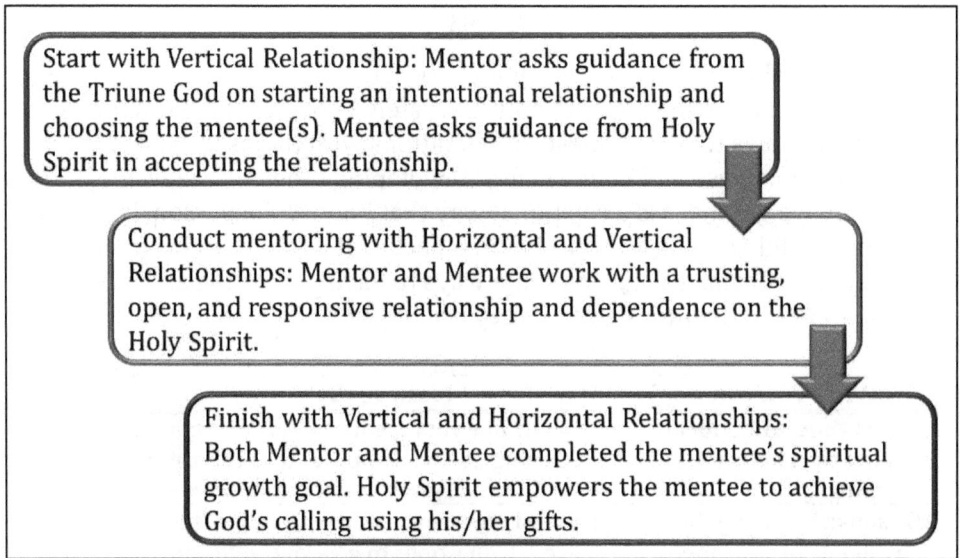

Start with Vertical Relationship: Mentor asks guidance from the Triune God on starting an intentional relationship and choosing the mentee(s). Mentee asks guidance from Holy Spirit in accepting the relationship.

Conduct mentoring with Horizontal and Vertical Relationships: Mentor and Mentee work with a trusting, open, and responsive relationship and dependence on the Holy Spirit.

Finish with Vertical and Horizontal Relationships: Both Mentor and Mentee completed the mentee's spiritual growth goal. Holy Spirit empowers the mentee to achieve God's calling using his/her gifts.

Figure 15-2. Relational Spiritual Mentorship Process[207]

Calderon then summarizes the interactive principles that make these mentoring relationships transformational.

> As a relational mentor, an interactive learning relationship with the participants was effective through (1) choosing and inviting the mentees with the leading of the Holy Spirit and praying for their acceptance to take the risk, (2) participating in the interactive modules for exchange of knowledge in understanding motivation and culture, (3) jointly designing the action plan, (4) equipping them with approaches for implementation individually and collectively, and (5) supporting their accountability efforts that will lead to or affirm transformational change individually and institutionally.[208]

> The character of a leader and mentor needs "high self-awareness, self-control, social awareness, and relationship management. They manage their emotions with transparency, adaptability, learning, initiative, and optimism. They have high empathy for the feelings of others and a great understanding of the relational dynamics of the community."[209]

---

[207] Rosario S. Calderon, "Spirit-Led Marketplace Transformation: Motivate, Equip, and Mobilize Filipino Christians in the San Francisco Bay Area" (Pre-publication Dissertation, Portland, OR, 2022), 138.

[208] Calderon, *Spirit-Led Marketplace Transformation*, 126.

[209] Wright, *Relational Leadership*. 69.

Depth

Mentoring relationships are designed to be trust-based connections where mentors and mentees can share deeply and safely with each other. Mentors encourage mentees to have honest conversations with themselves, with God, and with others. Reese and Loane state, "Developing others is a slow work – and the way we get there is a relational way that honors the person. It is a way that invites walking alongside another at a pace that allows for careful noticing to take place.[210] Zachary suggests some ways to have deepening and honest conversations with mentees, even if they are physically distant:

What you can do	Making the Connection
1. Invest time and effort in setting the climate for learning.	Determine your mentee's learning style and learning needs and how that might play out in your relationship, given that it is not face-to-face
2. Be sensitive to the day-to-day needs of your mentee.	Spend time connecting with your mentee. Ask enough questions to give you sufficient insight into his or her work context.
3. Identify and use multiple venues for communication.	Explore all available options: email, videoconference, e-learning technologies, telephone, mail, and emerging technology, and use more than one of these Look for opportunities to connect face-to-face, even at a long distance.
4. Set a regular contact schedule, but be flexible	Agree on a mutually convenient contact schedule, and make sure it works for you and your mentee. If you need to renegotiate a scheduled appointment, use that situation as an opportunity for connection and interaction.
5. Check on the effectiveness of your communication	.Ask questions: Are we connecting? Is what we are doing working for us? What can we do to improve the quality of our interaction?
6. Make sure that connection results in meaningful learning.	Is learning going on? Is the mentee making progress?
7. Share information and resources, but never as a substitute for personal interaction.	Set the stage to share information. The share the information and follow up.

Figure 15-3. Deepening Connections in Distance Mentoring[211]

---

[210] Reese and Loane, *Deep Mentoring*, 43.
[211] Zachary, *The Mentor's Guide*, 77.

Summary

In this chapter, we have examined the overlapping contexts that affect intercultural mentoring relationships, ways in which to intentionally structure the interaction that takes place between mentors and mentees, and some suggestions for helping the conversations take place at a deeply honest and transparent level. In the next chapter, we will focus on the transformation that is the goal of these interactions.

CHAPTER 16
Becoming in Intercultural Mentoring

The goal of the being, belonging, becoming process is transformational growth, as we influence each other to become more like Christ. That can be done in many contexts and settings, including intercultural mentoring settings. This chapter will focus on the transformational growth that people can experience within those relationships.

Influence

What influence do mentors seek to have on their mentees? It may be helpful to look at a couple of examples of contrasting lists to see what mentors try to help mentees avoid, and to attain. The first list is by Reese and Loane, who compare leaders who finish poorly with those who finish well, as shown in the figure below. Mentors can help mentees examine their values, character, and skills, to determine where weaknesses and strengths exist. Mentoring can then encourage the mentee to take appropriate action, in order to finish well.

Those who Finish Poorly	Those who Finish Well
• They misuse, mismanage, and abuse finances. • They struggle with issues of power. • They become trapped in their own pride. • They struggle with boundaries related to sex or issues of sexuality. • They fail to deal with family of origin issues. • They simply plateau in their development.	• They maintain a learning posture throughout life. • They value spiritual authority as a primary power base for leadership. • They recognize leadership selection and development as important. • They work from a dynamic and focused ministry philosophy. • They lead from a growing awareness of personal destiny. • They perceive their ministry from a lifetime perspective. • They prioritize mentoring relationships for themselves and in developing others.

Figure 16-1. Leaders Who Finish Poorly and Those Who Finish Well[212]

Edmund Chan writes, "The best mentors do not focus on the program but on the purpose," then emphasizes four principal objectives of mentoring, listed in the left hand column of the figure below. [213] The right hand column shows the learning domain or aspect of life that those objectives address.[214]

Objectives of Mentoring	Area of Life
Wisdom in thinking	Cognitive – what we think and how we think
Brokenness and humility in attitude	Affective – emotions and attitudes
Competence in life-skills and ministry-skills	Behavioral –actions
Experience of God's power and presence.	Dispositional- character that has been transformed by God

Figure 16-2. Key Objectives of Mentoring

Transgressional Decline

Not all changes in our lives are positive. Pue lists spiritual danger zones in leadership that fall into the 'transgressional decline' end of the 'becoming' spectrum that we illustrated in Figure 2-7. These are areas that can be identified and addressed through mentoring:

- Reliance on own gifts
- Fear of humankind (people pleasing)
- Perfectionism
- Lack of conflict resolution skills or avoidance of conflict
- Lack of accountability
- Ignoring evil or lack of understanding how evil works
- Unawareness of how to guard against sexual misconduct
- Empire building
- Need for recognition
- Need to control
- Lack of trust / intimacy with God (solitude, etc.)

---

[212] Reese and Loane, *Deep Mentoring*, 225–31.
[213] Chan, *Mentoring Paradigms*, 46–48.
[214] Shaw, *Transforming Theological Education*, 69.

- Inability to set boundaries (to say no)
- Inability to delegate
- Lack of discernment[215]

Transformational Growth

Robert Clinton defines the spiritual or character formation process as "the development of the inner life of a person of God so that the person

1. experiences more of God,
2. reflects more God-like characteristics in personality and everyday relationships, and
3. increasingly knows the power and presence of God in ministry."[216]

These are all areas that can profitably be addressed by mentoring, to aid in positive transformational growth as we have defined it. Let us examine a few representative areas of issues that mentors may need to address as they help their mentors grow. Since mentoring is a reciprocal process, mentees may also help their mentors to grow in these areas.

Spiritual Maturity

Character formation, or spiritual maturity, is a key focus in a mentoring relationship. Reese and Loane comment, "If we are going to walk closely with women and men who are early in their leadership development, then their giftedness or insight must not fool us. We must recognize that their character is key over the long haul."[217] Christ-like character involves growing in humility, obedience, holiness, and faithfulness.

Two of the central elements of spiritual maturity are

humble obedience to God, and humble service to others. Philippians 2:3-8 is a familiar passage, but one which is difficult to practice. Mentors and mentees can encourage each other to grow in this area:

Do nothing from selfish ambition or conceit, but in humility count others more significant than yourselves. Let each of you look not only to his own interests, but also to the interests of others. Have this mind among yourselves, which is yours in Christ Jesus, who, though he was in the form of

---

[215] Pue, *Mentoring Leaders*, 51.

[216] Reese and Loane, *Deep Mentoring*, 135, based on material in J. Robert Clinton, *The Making of a Leader* (Colorado Springs: NavPress, 1988), 255. Formatting changed for emphasis.

[217] Reese and Loane, 112.

God, did not count equality with God a thing to be grasped, but emptied himself, by taking the form of a servant, being born in the likeness of men. And being found in human form, he humbled himself by becoming obedient to the point of death, even death on a cross.

Holiness and faithfulness are also important aspects of spiritual maturity. I Peter 1:14-16 states, "As obedient children, do not conform to the evil desires you had when you lived in ignorance. But just as he who called you is holy, so be holy in all you do; for it is written: "Be holy, because I am holy." Reese and Loane state, "If we are concerned with the leadership formation of others, and if we desire to imitate Jesus' way, then we must pay attention with a seeing heart to those around us."[218] They pose a key question that needs to be answered by everyone involved in mentoring relationships. "How then are we actually helping people to mature into lives of greater compassion, integrity, wisdom and service in Jesus' name?"[219]

Emphasizing 'organization' over 'organism' can distract individuals, churches, and other groups from pursuing holiness and faithfulness. While a church is both an organization and an organism, Reese and Loane warn against the problem of "substituting techniques and technology for love".[220]

Emphasis on relationship

This book has sought to emphasize the importance of relationship in the process of transformational growth, and to provide suggestions and illustrations of how that might be accomplished in various setting. Pue states the goal this way: "It is interesting to contemplate what God might do if we were to throw ourselves into developing co-workers for the sake of bringing them into a closer relationship with Jesus."[221]

Chan states, "Mentoring is an impartation of life and convictions. It is about living a life and sharing the journey. It also involves imparting values and vision, creating a new empowering belief system. All this takes time. It involves a complex process of growth. And growth takes time. And skill."[222] One way of emphasizing relationships in and through mentoring is to consider using mentoring teams. This could be teams of mentors who each help mentees with

---

[218] Reese and Loane, *Deep Mentoring*, 35.

[219] Reese and Loane, *Deep Mentoring*, 37.

[220] Reese and Loane, *Deep Mentoring*, 40, quoting James M. Houston, *Letters of Faith Through the Seasons* (Colorado Springs; Cook, 2006), 1:175.

[221] Pue, *Mentoring Leaders*, 210.

[222] Chan, *Mentoring Paradigms*, 58.

various areas of growth over a period of time, or a ministry team which receives mentoring together from a mentor or team of mentors.

A mentoring relationship might become a long-term connection, but that is not a requirement in order for mentoring to be beneficial. Zachary states, "Today's mentoring relationships are usually short term; when the learning goals have been accomplished, the relationship comes to closure. If goals have not been achieved by a prearranged deadline or the partners agree on more goals, the mentoring partners are free to review, assess, and renegotiate their relationship.[223] It is important, in fact, that a follow-up and evaluation system is in place; along with a plan for any ongoing mentoring.

Vision and Goals

Having vision for their group or organization can be an important issue for a mentee. This does not mean that every step and process is clearly set and unchangeable, but it gives a desired view of the future. Sherwood Lingenfelter links vision with "an understanding of what the Scriptures teach of the kingdom of God and the vision that flows out of the power of the Holy Spirit to establish that kingdom now and in the ages to come."[224] Vision is part of trying to see our part in God's over-arching story of history, and what God may be planning to do in and through us in the future. Lingenfelter states, "God's mission and vision requires our obedience, as we first listen to the Holy Spirit, obey by taking the first steps, and then share that vision with others".[225]

Pue addresses two fundamental principles to consider as we mentor in the area vision:

1   *God is the instiller of vision.* There are too many conferences we attend and books on the shelves of our libraries and bookstores that reduce vision to some kind of personal exercise and discipline. We can help leaders by pointing them back to the vision stories found in the Bible and asking them to study how God went about instilling vision and what his purposes were in doing so.
2   *God is also sovereign.* He can change plans and even change vision, especially if leaders are not ready and need to grow before they can embrace the fullness of his vision for their life.[226]

---

[223] Zachary, *Mentor's Guide*, 25.
[224] Sherwood G. Lingenfelter. *Leading Cross-Culturally: Covenant Relationships for Effective Christian Leadership.* (Grand Rapids, MI: Baker Academic, 2008), 31.
[225] Lingenfelter, *Leading Cross-Culturally*, 33.
[226] Pue, *Mentoring Leaders*, 128.

Mentors can model how to discern God's wisdom in the Scriptures, through prayer, and through wise counsel. In doing so, they can help their mentees do the same.

Dealing with conflict.

Conflict is inevitable in ministry and in life. It can also be a good incentive for growth in a person's life. Pue states:

> Christian leaders need to understand that they will have times in their leadership when maintaining harmonious human relations is simply not possible. Trying to be "nice" leaves people not really knowing where they stand. Not confronting or giving feedback to those we work with in ministry allows them to keep making the same mistakes – something that is not helpful to them or the ministry.[227]

If conflict arises in the mentoring relationship, the mentor's response can serve as a positive example for how the mentee can lead through conflict in the future.

The Ripple Effect of Influence

We have now explored the process that repeats across time of individuals (beings) connecting and interacting together (belonging), and having reciprocal influence on each other (becoming). It is helpful to recall Figure 2-10 (repeated below), which discussed the role that individual choice has on the influences that we are surrounded by.

---

[227] Pue, *Mentoring Leaders*, 195.

Choice	Godliness	Reject ungodly influence, resulting in transformational change	Accept godly influence, resulting in transformational change
	Ungodliness	Accept ungodly influence, resulting in transgressional change	Reject godly influence, resulting in transgressional change
		Ungodliness	**Godliness**
		Influence	

Figure 16-3. The Roles of Influence and Choice

We can use ungodly influences to motivate us toward godliness, as God uses evil intentions to produce good results (Genesis 50: 20). Alternatively, we can choose to rebel against good influences in our lives, resulting in ungodliness. As mentors and mentees influence each other, the goal is that both the influence and the choices that the individuals make will result in godliness.

Godly influence within mentoring extends past that relationship and affects others as well. We have looked at the impact that leadership and discipleship can have on those who are not in direct relationship with the original leader or discipler. The same is true of mentors, as shown in the following figure. The interactions that take place in the being-belonging-becoming process also influence others who are also in their own stages of transformational growth. The interactions between a mentor and mentees also influence the interactions between mentees and others, both inside and outside of the faith community.

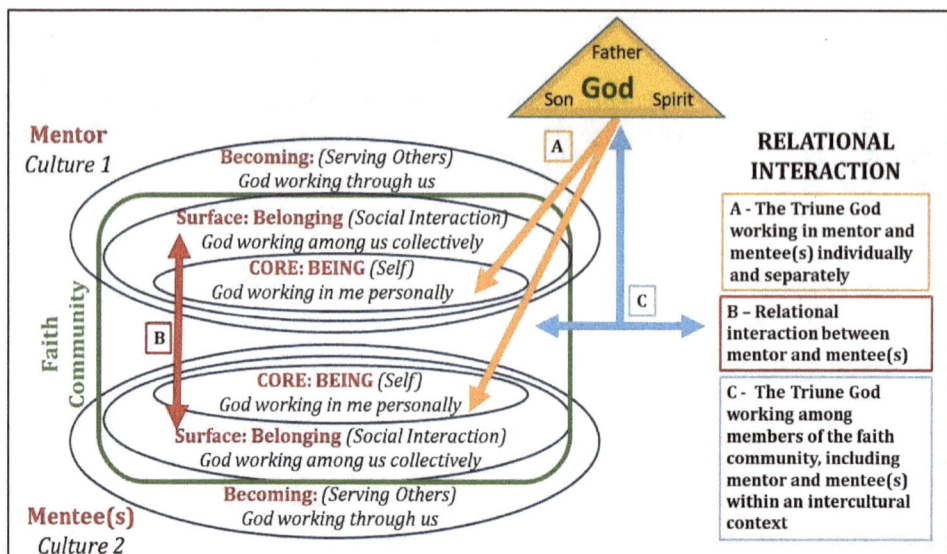

Figure 16-4. Intercultural Mentorship in Action

The ripple effect of influence should motivate us to be deliberate in our mentoring relationships (and in all of our relationships), to strive to be a godly influence, and to encourage and pray for those who we influence directly and indirectly, to choose transformative growth and godliness. Romans 12, for example, give us a glimpse at some of these interactions that affect a variety of individuals through a network of connections. Paul begins this passage with the well-known passage related to transformation:

> Therefore, I urge you, brothers and sisters, in view of God's mercy, to offer your bodies as a living sacrifice, holy and pleasing to God—this is your true and proper worship. Do not conform to the pattern of this world, but be transformed by the renewing of your mind. Then you will be able to test and approve what God's will is—his good, pleasing and perfect will. (Romans 12:1-2)

While the 'you' pronouns here are plural, the commands to not be conformed but to be transformed are actions which individual believers are responsible to carry out. This is particularly clear in the following verse: "For by the grace given me I say to every one of you: Do not think of yourself more highly than you ought, but rather think of yourself with sober judgment, in accordance with the faith God has distributed to each of you" (Romans 12:3). Each person is responsible, in cooperation with the Holy Spirit, for developing their vertical relationship with God, and for fostering their own attitudes. This reflects some of the aspects of "God working in me personally" as shown in the 'core' circle.

160

Paul then focus on gifts, attitudes, and actions that promote unity and love within the church body. These verses describe interactions that take place between individuals and within group settings that are the evidence of God working within His children collectively:

For just as each of us has one body with many members, and these members do not all have the same function, so in Christ we, though many, form one body, and each member belongs to all the others. We have different gifts, according to the grace given to each of us. If your gift is prophesying, then prophesy in accordance with your faith; if it is serving, then serve; if it is teaching, then teach; if it is to encourage, then give encouragement; if it is giving, then give generously; if it is to lead, do it diligently; if it is to show mercy, do it cheerfully. Love must be sincere. Hate what is evil; cling to what is good. Be devoted to one another in love. Honor one another above yourselves. Never be lacking in zeal, but keep your spiritual fervor, serving the Lord. Be joyful in hope, patient in affliction, faithful in prayer. Share with the Lord's people who are in need. Practice hospitality (Romans 12:4-13)

In the rest of the chapter, Paul looks outside of the church, to encourage godly attitudes and actions toward non-believers. This is indicated by references to persecutors, God's wrath, and enemies:

Bless those who persecute you; bless and do not curse. Rejoice with those who rejoice; mourn with those who mourn. Live in harmony with one another. Do not be proud, but be willing to associate with people of low position. Do not be conceited. Do not repay anyone evil for evil. Be careful to do what is right in the eyes of everyone. If it is possible, as far as it depends on you, live at peace with everyone. Do not take revenge, my dear friends, but leave room for God's wrath, for it is written: "It is mine to avenge; I will repay," says the Lord. On the contrary: "If your enemy is hungry, feed him; if he is thirsty, give him something to drink. In doing this, you will heap burning coals on his head." Do not be overcome by evil, but overcome evil with good (Romans 12:14-21).

In these verses, and continuing into chapter 13, where Paul discusses obedience to civil authorities, he explores those spheres of influence that believers have outside of our relationships with fellow believers. He emphasizes the importance of doing what is right (verse 17) and of overcoming evil with good (verse 21). This is consistent with the emphasis in Figure 16-4 for us to allow God to work through us in service to those outside of the faith community. As mentors and mentees, we can be deliberate about the interactions we have with individuals inside and outside of the church, and the potential godly influence we can have on them. And we can be praying for them as they cooperate with the Holy Spirt to impact others who are outside of our own spheres of influence.

Summary

Mentoring is a relationship that can bring individual beings into contact with each other through intentional conversations that are designed to help produce transformational growth. It can be challenging to be involved in such a relationship, especially when mentors and mentees bring different cultural perspectives and expectations. But God is able to direct and empower the relationship and all of its interactions, and use them to produce the results he intends. As Philippians 1:6 states, "being confident of this, that he who began a good work in you will carry it on to completion until the day of Christ Jesus."

CHAPTER 17
Intercultural Mentoring Summary

We have looked at what the process of being, belonging, and becoming might look like in and through a mentoring relationship. We invite you to think through that process in the following scenario. Enoch Wan and John Ferch describe a mentoring relationship between an experienced pastor or missionary and a disciple or leader in training in an Inuit context:

> A pastor may not feel qualified to train in person in the intricacies of exegesis or homiletics, but these matters of "content" can easily be left to specialized instructors. Instead, the pastor or missionary can focus on engaging disciples in day-to-day ministry activities and basic study of the Scriptures. Taking a younger disciple along when visiting the sick or participating in denominational conferences, for example, will provide valuable ministry experience that can translate into a leadership role in the future. A consistent pattern of mentoring meetings between the disciple and the local mentor form the backbone of the relational model. These meetings ought to emphasize in equal parts study (oral study of the Scriptures) and practice (ministry activities such as teaching, pastoral care, and visitation.[228]

- **Being:** In this setting, who are the people present? How might their cultural perspectives differ? What might the needs of the disciple or mentee be? How might the Persons, character, and power of the Triune God be an intentional focus in this relationship?
- **Belonging**: What are the various cultural, personal, and environmental contexts that might be present? How might the mentor shape the interactions to be transformative? How could each person help with the depth and transparency of the conversations?
- **Becoming**: How might the mentor and mentee(s) each help the others grow in each of the following areas: spiritual, social, moral, intellectual, emotional, and physical? How might readiness and timing be a factor in that growth?
- **Application**: How might you answer these questions for a relationship the Lord has called to you into? What other questions would you ask?

---

[228] Enoch Wan and John Ferch, *Relational Leadership Development: An Ethnological Study in Inuit Contexts* (Portland, OR: Western Academic Publishers, 2022), 103.

CHAPTER 18
Conclusion

For those relationships where you are engaged in intercultural leading, discipling, or mentoring, we pray that God will use you to help in the transformation process of making people more into the image of God the Son. And we invite you to explore ways of being intentional to facilitate transformational growth through the connections, interactions, and influences that you have in your other relationships. In the words of Colossians 1:9b-14, may God...

> fill you with the knowledge of his will through all the wisdom and understanding that the Spirit gives, so that you may live a life worthy of the Lord and please him in every way: bearing fruit in every good work, growing in the knowledge of God, being strengthened with all power according to his glorious might so that you may have great endurance and patience, and giving joyful thanks to the Father, who has qualified you to share in the inheritance of his holy people in the kingdom of light. For he has rescued us from the dominion of darkness and brought us into the kingdom of the Son he loves, in whom we have redemption, the forgiveness of sins.

BIBLIOGRAPHY

Bennett, Milton J. "Towards Ethnorelativism: A Developmental Model of Intercultural Sensitivity." In *Education for the Intercultural Experience*, 21–71. Yarmouth, ME: Intercultural Press, Inc., 1993.

Bradshaw, Bruce. *Change across Cultures: A Narrative Approach to Social Transformation*. Grand Rapids: Baker Academic, 2002.

Brookfield, Stephen D. "Transformative Learning as Ideology Critique." In *Learning as Transformation: Critical Perspectives on a Theory in Progress*, 125–48. San Francisco: Jossey-Bass, 2000.

Bruce, A. B. *The Training of the Twelve: How Jesus Christ Found and Taught the 12 Apostles; A Book of New Testament Biography*. CreateSpace Independent Publishing Platform, 2018.

———. *The Training of the Twelve: How Jesus Christ Found and Taught the 12 Apostles; A Book of New Testament Biography*. Second edition. Grand Rapids: Christian Classics Ethereal Library. Accessed January 9, 2023. https://www.nobts.edu/discipleship/downloadable-documents1/leadership-folder/The%20Trainin%20of%20the%20Twelve.pdf.

Calderon, Rosario S. "Spirit-Led Marketplace Transformation: Motivate, Equip, and Mobilize Filipino Christians in the San Francisco Bay Area." Pre-publication Dissertation, 2022.

Cartwright, John, Gabriel Etzel, Christopher Jackson, and Timothy Paul Jones. *Teaching the World: Foundations for Online Theological Education*. Nashville: B&H Academic, 2017.

Chan, Edmund. *Mentoring Paradigms: Reflections on Mentoring, Leadership, and Discipleship*. Oklahoma City: Lifestyle Impact Publishing, 2008.

Chiu, Ai Chen (Noel). "Key Parameters of Establishing Frontline LGBTQ Outreach." Doctor of Education, Western Seminary, 2021.

Curran, Timothy, Kerry Copeland, Enanga Daisy Fale, Richenal M. Jr. Martin, and Laura McIntyre. "The Effect of Personality on Mentoring." *The Chronicle of Mentoring & Coaching* 1, no. Special Issue 10 (December 2017): 381–87.

Darby, Flower, and James M. Lang. *Small Teaching Online: Applying Learning Science in Online Classes*. First edition. San Francisco, CA: Jossey-Bass, 2019.

Edwards, Mark J. *Galatians, Ephesians, Philippians*. Ancient Christian Commentary on Scripture. Downers Grove, IL: InterVarsity Press, 1999.

Foulkes, Francis. *The Letter of Paul to the Ephesians: An Introduction and Commentary*. 2nd edition. Leicester, England : Grand Rapids, MI: Eerdmans Pub Co, 1989.

Gimple, Ryan, and Enoch Wan. *Covenant Transformative Learning: Theory and Practice.* Portland, Oregon: Western Seminary Press, 2021.

Growing Together: A Three-Part Guide for Following Jesus and Bringing Friends on the Journey. The Barna Group, 2022.

Hannaford, Ronald G. "A Model of Online Education Effecting Holistic Student Formation Appropriate for Global Cross-Cultural Contexts." Fuller Theological Seminary, 2012.

Hedinger, Mark. *Culture Learning: The Art of Understanding What No One Can Teach You.* Portland, OR: CultureBound, 2021.

Hibbert, Evelyn, and Richard Hibbert. *Walking Together On The Jesus Road: Intercultural Discipling.* Littleton, CO: William Carey Library, 2018.

Hiebert, Paul G. "Conversion and Worldview Transformation." *International Journal of Frontier Missions* 14, no. 2 (June 1997): 83–86.

Hiebert, Paul G., and Eloise Hiebert Meneses. *Incarnational Ministry: Planting Churches in Band, Tribal, Peasant, and Urban Societies.* Grand Rapids: Baker Books, 1995.

Hinde, Robert A. *Relationships: A Dialectical Perspective.* London, U.K.: Psychology Press, 1997.

Hofstede, Geert. "The 6 Dimensions Model of National Culture." Geert Hofstede. Accessed February 1, 2023. https://geerthofstede.com/culture-geert-hofstede-gert-jan-hofstede/6d-model-of-national-culture/.

Jamieson, Robert, A. R. Fausset, and David Brown. *Commentary Practical and Explanatory on the Whole Bible.* 2nd Printing. Oak Harbor, WA: Zondervan Publishing House, 1962.

Jensenius, Alexander Refsum. "Disciplinarities: Intra, Cross, Multi, Inter, Trans." *ARJ (English)* (blog), March 12, 2012. https://www.arj.no/2012/03/12/disciplinarities-2/.

Johnson, Andy. "Pragmatism, Pragmatism Everywhere!" *9Marks* (blog), February 2, 2010. https://www.9marks.org/article/pragmatism-pragmatism-everywhere/.

Kolb, Alice Y., and David A. Kolb. "The Kolb Learning Style Inventory Version 3.1: 2005 Technical Specifications." Hay Resources Direct, 2005.

Lawrence, James. *Growing Leaders: Cultivating Discipleship for Yourself and Others.* Peabody, MA: Hendrickson Publishers, Inc., 2004.

Lingenfelter, Judith E., and Sherwood G. Lingenfelter. *Teaching Cross-Culturally: An Incarnational Model for Learning and Teaching.* Grand Rapids: Baker Academic, 2003.

Lowe, Stephen D., and Mary E. Lowe. *Ecologies of Faith in a Digital Age: Spiritual Growth through Online Education.* Downer's Grove: IVP Academic, 2018.

———. "Spiritual Formation in Theological Distance Education: An Ecosystems Model." *Christian Education Journal*, 3, 7 (2010): 85–102.

Meek, Esther Lightcap. *Loving to Know: Introducing Covenant Epistemology.* Eugene, OR: Cascade Books, 2011.

Mesquita, Batja. *Between Us: How Cultures Create Emotions.* New York, NY: W. W. Norton & Company, 2022.

———. *Between Us: How Cultures Create Emotions.* New York, NY: W. W. Norton & Company, 2022.

Mezirow, Jack. "How Critical Reflection Triggers Transformative Learning." In *Fostering Critical Reflection in Adulthood: A Guide to Transformative and Emancipatory Learning*, 1–20. San Francisco, CA: Jossey-Bass, 1990.

———. *Learning as Transformation: Critical Perspectives on a Theory in Progress.* San Francisco: Jossey-Bass, 2000.

———. *Learning as Transformation: Critical Perspectives on a Theory in Progress.* 1st ed. The Jossey-Bass Higher and Adult Education Series. San Francisco: Jossey-Bass, 2000.

———. "Learning to Think Like an Adult: Core Concepts of Transformation Theory." In *Learning as Transformation: Critical Perspectives on a Theory in Progress*, 3–33. San Francisco: Jossey-Bass, 2000.

———. "Transformative Learning as Discourse." *Journal of Transformative Education* 1, no. 1 (January 2003): 58–63.

Moon, W. Jay. *Intercultural Discipleship: Learning from Global Approaches to Spiritual Formation.* Grand Rapids: Baker Academic, 2017.

———. *Intercultural Discipleship: Learning from Global Approaches to Spiritual Formation.* Grand Rapids, Michigan: Baker Academic, 2017.

Ogden, Greg. *Transforming Discipleship: Making Disciples a Few at a Time.* Revised and Expanded. Downers Grove, IL: IVP Books, 2016.

Osula, Bramwell, and Steve M. Irvin. "Cultural Awareness in Intercultural Mentoring: A Model for Enhancing Mentoring Relationships." *International Journal of Leadership Studies, School of Global Leadership & Entrepreneurship, Regent University* 5, no. 1 (2009): 37–50.

Ott, Craig. *Teaching and Learning across Cultures: A Guide to Theory and Practice.* Grand Rapids, MI: Baker Academic, 2021.

Pazmiño, Robert W. *Foundational Issues in Christian Education: An Introduction in Evangelical Perspective.* 3rd edition. Grand Rapids, MI: Baker Academic, 2008.

———. *God Our Teacher: Theological Basics in Christian Education.* Eugene, OR: Wipf and Stock, 2016.

Peckham, Jeremy. "Relational Leadership." *Evangelical Focus* (blog), April 12, 2016. http://evangelicalfocus.com/blogs/1527/Relational_Leadership.

Penner, Robert. "Kingdom Citizens on Mission: A Missiological Reading of Matthew's Gospel for Missionary Preparation." Western Seminary, 2017.

Plueddemann, James E. *Leading Across Cultures: Effective Ministry and Mission in the Global Church.* Downers Grove, IL: IVP Academic, 2009.

———. *Teaching Across Cultures: Contextualizing Education for Global Mission.* Downers Grove, IL: IVP Academic, 2018.

Pue, Carson. *Mentoring Leaders: Wisdom for Developing Character, Calling, and Competency.* Grand Rapids: Baker Books, 2005.

Raibley, Jon. "Experiencing Communities of Learning: A Phenomenological Study of Students Enrolled in Western Seminary's Online Master of Divinity Program." Western Seminary, 2021.

Reese, Randy D., and Robert Loane. *Deep Mentoring: Guiding Others on Their Leadership Journey.* Downers Grove, IL: Inter-Varsity Press, 2012.

Shaw, Perry. *Transforming Theological Education: A Practical Handbook for Integrative Learning.* Carlisle, Cumbria UK: Lanham Partnership, 2014.

Snode, Travis. "Mentoring in the New Testament (5 of 5) – Paul and Timothy." *Into All The World* (blog), November 6, 2013. https://www.travissnode.com/articles/leadership/mentoring-new-testament-5-5-paul-timothy/.

———. "Mentoring in the Old Testament (7 of 7) – Elijah and Elisha." *Into All The World* (blog), September 18, 2013. https://www.travissnode.com/articles/leadership/mentoring-old-testament-7-7-elijah-elisha/.

Stember, Marilyn. "Advancing the Social Sciences through the Interdisciplinary Enterprise." *The Social Science Journal* 28, no. 1 (1991): 1–14. https://doi.org/10.1016/0362-3319(91)90040-B.

Stott, John. *The Message of Ephesians: God's New Society.* Revised edition. The Bible Speaks Today. Downers Grove, IL: IVP, 2020.

Thaler, Richard H., and Cass R. Sunstein. *Nudge: Improving Decisions about Health, Wealth, and Happiness.* London: Yale University Press, 2008.

Theopulos. "Paul and Timothy." Fuller Seminary. *The Next Faithful Step* (blog), 2019. https://www.fuller.edu/next-faithful-step/resources/paul-and-timothy/.

Thomas, Matt. "The Indispensable Mark of Christian Leadership: Implications from Christ's Methods of Leadership Development in Mark's Gospel." *Perichoresis* 16, no. 3 (June 30, 2018): 107–17. https://doi.org/10.2478/perc-2018-0019.

Trompenaars, Fons, and Charles Hampden-Turner. *Riding the Waves of Culture: Understanding Diversity in Global Business.* Third edition. New York: McGraw-Hill, 2012.

Wan, Enoch. "A Theological Reflection on Inter-Cultural Reality and Intercultural Education." Unpublished material. Portland, OR, 2020.

———. "Issues and Practice Related to Intercultural Education: IE701 Lecture PowerPoint Notes," March 2021.

———. "Narrative Framework for Relational Transformational Growth." Presented at the Evangelical Missiological Society National Conference, Virtual, September 2021.

———. "Relational Intercultural Leadership and Mentorship." Unpublished material, February 14, 2022.

———. "Relational Transformation Leadership - An Asian Christian Perspective." *Asian Missions Advance*, April 2021. http://www.asiamissions.net/relational-transformational-leadership-an-asian-christian-perspective/.

———. "Relational Transformational Leadership — An Asian Christian Perspective." *Asian Missions Advance*, 2021. http://www.asiamissions.net/asian-missions-advances/.

———. "Rethinking Urban Mission in Terms of Spiritual and Social Transformational Change." Presented at the Missiological Society of Ghana/WAMS Biennial International Conference, Virtual, October 26, 2021.

———. "The Paradigm of 'Relational Realism.'" *Occasional Bulletin* 19, no. 2 (Spring 2006): 4.

Wan, Enoch, and Howard Chen. *Marketplace Transformation: Motivating and Mobilizing Chinese Churches in the Silicon Valley for Gospel Transformation.* Portland, Oregon: Western Press, 2021.

———. *Marketplace Transformation: Motivating and Mobilizing Chinese Churches in the Silicon Valley for Gospel Transformation.* Portland, Oregon: Western Press, 2021.

Wan, Enoch, and John Ferch. *Relational Leadership Development: An Ethnological Study in Inuit Contexts.* Portland, OR: Western Academic Publishers, 2022.

Wan, Enoch, and John Jay Flinn. *Holistic Mission through Mission Partnership: An Instrumental Case Study in La Ceiba, Honduras.* Western Academic Publishers, 2021.

Wan, Enoch, and Mark Hedinger. *Relational Missionary Training.* Urban Ministry in the 21st Century. Skycrest, CA: Urban Loft Publishers, 2017.

———. "Transformative Ministry for the Majority World Context; Applying Relational Approaches." *Occasional Bulletin* 31, no. 2 (Spring 2018): 4–17, 47.

Wan, Enoch, and Natalie Kim. *Relational Intercultural Training for Practitioners of Business As Mission: Theory and Practice.* Western Academic Publishers, 2022.

Wan, Enoch, and Jon Raibley. *Transformational Change in Christian Ministry.* Second Edition. Portland, Oregon: Western Academic Publishers, 2022.

171

———. "Transforming Meaning Perspectives and Intercultural Education." In *Covenant Transformative Learning Theory and Practice for Mission*, 147–62. Western Seminary Press, 2021.

Wright, Walter C. Jr. *Mentoring: The Promise of Relational Leadership*. 2006 Reprint. Milton Keynes, Bucks, UK: Paternoster Press, 2004.

———. *Relational Leadership: A Biblical Model for Influence and Service*. Second edition. Downers Grove, IL: IVP Books, 2009.

Zachary, Lois J. *The Mentor's Guide: Facilitating Effective Learning Relationships*. Second. San Francisco: Jossey-Bass, 2012.